PENGUIN WRITERS' GUIDES

How to Write Effective Emails

R. L. TRASK

PENGUIN BOOKS

D0057410

PENGUIN BOOKS

Published by the Penguin Group
Penguin Books Ltd, 80 Strand, London WC2R 0RL, England
Penguin Group (USA) Inc., 375 Hudson Street, New York, New York 10014, USA
Penguin Group (Canada), 10 Alcorn Avenue, Toronto, Ontario, Canada M4V 3B2
(a division of Pearson Penguin Canada Inc.)
Penguin Ireland, 25 St Stephen's Green, Dublin 2, Ireland
(a division of Penguin Books Ltd)
Penguin Group (Australia), 250 Camberwell Road,
Camberwell, Victoria 3124, Australia (a division of Pearson Australia Group Pty Ltd)
Penguin Books India Pvt Ltd, 11 Community Centre,
Panchsheel Park, New Delhi – 110 017, India
Penguin Group (NZ), cnr Airborne and Rosedale Roads, Albany,
Auckland 1310, New Zealand (a division of Pearson New Zealand Ltd)
Penguin Books (South Africa) (Pty) Ltd, 24 Sturdee Avenue,
Rosebank 2196, South Africa

Penguin Books Ltd, Registered Offices: 80 Strand, London WC2R 0RL, England

www.penguin.com

First published 2005
2

Set in 11/13 pt Adobe Minion
Typeset by Rowland Phototypesetting Ltd, Bury St Edmunds, Suffolk
Printed in England by Clays Ltd, St Ives plc

PENGUIN WRITERS' GUIDES

How to Write Effective Emails

R. L. Trask was born in western New York State in 1944. Having come to England in 1970, he obtained his Ph.D. from the University of London in 1983. He taught linguistics at the University of Liverpool from 1979 to 1988, and then at the School of Cognitive and Computing Science (now the Linguistics and English Language Department) at the University of Sussex. His special interests were historical linguistics, grammar and the Basque language. He wrote a number of books, including *A Dictionary of Grammatical Terms in Linguistics*, *Language Change*, *Language: The Basics*, *The Penguin Guide to Punctuation*, *The Penguin Dictionary of English Grammar* and *Mind the Gaffe*. *How to Write Effective Emails* is sadly his last book for Penguin as he died in 2004.

The Penguin Writers' Guides

For my wonderful Jan

Contents

Acknowledgements

For advice on various points, I am indebted to Marion Brooker, Nick Brooker, Richard Coates, Emily Ellerton, Jan Lock, Lynne Murphy, Geoffrey Sampson, Patrick Warren and Max Wheeler.

While writing this book, I consulted dozens of web pages offering advice on email. The ones which I found particularly helpful were those constructed by Jim Britell (*http://www.britell.com/use/use19.html*), Sally Hambridge (*http://www.dtcc.edu/cs/rfc1855.html*) and Kaitlin Duck Sherwood (*http://www.webfoot.com/advice/email.top.html*). All were consulted in January 2003.

Any shortcomings are my own responsibility.

1
What This Book Is For

1.1 WHY THIS BOOK?

More and more of us are spending more and more time sending and receiving emails. If you're looking at this book, then you are probably already deep into the world of electronic mail. Some of your emails are probably informal chit-chat with close friends or with fellow hobbyists, but others are different. Sometimes you send an email to somebody you don't know at all, looking for advice or assistance. And sometimes you send emails to business colleagues, with the intention of getting some work done. And that's what this book is for.

When you mail a friend or a fellow enthusiast, you can use your own judgement as to what style is best, and you may choose a casual and chatty style, perhaps even a jokey one. But, when you approach a stranger or a business associate, things are utterly different. Now, a casual and chatty style is dead wrong, and a very different style is called for.

The purpose of this book is to help you to write

effective emails when you deal with strangers and business colleagues. When you are looking for advice or assistance, or when you are conducting any kind of serious business electronically, you want to make the best possible impression on the people you are mailing. You want them to see that you are mature, businesslike and professional, and you want them to conclude that your mail should be taken seriously. You do *not* want to give them the impression that you are dopey, irresponsible or immature, that you are merely a child fooling around with a new toy.

Writing effective emails is not a trivial task. Just like learning anything worthwhile, learning to write good emails takes time, attention and effort. You need to pay attention to what you are doing, to think about whether you are doing the right thing, and to put a good deal of effort into what you write.

Email has been around long enough now that a body of conventions has grown up concerning what is courteous and proper. These conventions are commonly known as **Netiquette**, a cute neologism for 'etiquette on the Internet'. If you want your emails to be taken seriously, then it is vital that you respect the conventions of Netiquette. And teaching you those conventions is the purpose of this book.

Judging by the large number of truly awful emails I receive every week, I conclude that there are a lot of people out there who have not yet understood the importance of learning to write emails properly. Astonishingly, there are even a few professionals who have not understood this.

Now and again, I have encountered a professional

giving out this advice: 'Write emails in the manner you use in speaking casually, since it is rude to compose them with the formal conventions of other types of writing.' This is *terrible* advice, and I can only conclude that the people who give it must receive all their email from another planet.

Perhaps once or twice a year I receive an email which is uncomfortably stiff and formal – but that's only because the writer's stiff and stuffy personality is spilling over into his writing. But I get hundreds and hundreds of emails which are far too casual to be effective, and not just casual, but careless, sloppy, childish – and rude.

It is very hard to be rude by being formal and careful in your writing. But it is extremely easy to give offence if you fail to take sufficient care with your writing. I can demonstrate this by pointing to my email inbox on any day of the year. Later in this book, I will be showing you lots of examples of terrible emails.

Anyway, email is a form of writing, and it suffers from the same problems as all other forms of writing. When we talk, we communicate in all sorts of ways besides the words we are using. We use intonation, tempo, volume, pitch and stress – in other words, tone of voice – and we further use postures, gestures and expressions. All these things contribute substantially to the meanings we convey, and they help us to avoid obscurity and misunderstanding. Moreover, if obscurity or misunderstanding *does* occur in speech, we usually notice it at once, and we take steps to fix things.

None of this is true of writing. *All* of these valuable clues are lost in writing, and there is no possibility of spotting or repairing any misunderstandings. This is just as true of emails as it is of any other kind of writing. Accordingly, if we fail to write our emails with great care, we risk all kinds of misunderstanding and confusion. Writing on a computer screen instead of a sheet of paper does nothing to make these problems go away. And pretending that email is just an electronic version of conversation is a terrible mistake.

1.2 INFORMALITY

It is commonly said that email is an 'informal' medium. This statement is true, up to a point, but it is often badly misunderstood.

When I compose an email, I don't write it in the kind of formal English I would use in writing a learned article for a scholarly journal. For example, I use the pronouns *I* and *you* freely in my emails, but I don't use them in my formal writing. My emails sometimes contain incomplete sentences like *Not so*, but these never occur in my formal writing. In an email, I might find occasion to mention my wife or my friends, or to relate an anecdote about something that happened to me once, or to say something about recent political events. I wouldn't do any of these things in my scholarly writing.

To this extent, then, email is 'informal'. The style which is appropriate for emails is not the style appropriate for the most formal kinds of writing.

But 'informal' does not mean 'casual'. It does not mean 'hasty'. It does not mean 'sloppy'. It does not mean 'cutesy and jokey'. It does not mean 'departing from standard English'. It does not mean 'ignoring common courtesy'. It does not mean 'resembling the personal letters of an eleven-year-old schoolgirl'. When I say that emails are 'informal', I most certainly do not mean that they should be thrown together in moments and then fired off without being edited or even proofread.

Sadly, the constant advice from some quarters to keep emails 'informal' has very often had the unintended effect of producing all of these dreadful outcomes. I know, because precisely those dreadful outcomes arrive in my inbox every day of the week.

Just to cite one example, many people commit the terrible blunder of failing to sign their emails. I get a dozen or two unsigned emails every week. Recently I asked the woman who had sent me one of them why she had failed to sign her name. She replied that she had been advised that email was an 'informal' medium, and she was afraid that signing her mail would be unacceptably 'formal'.

Well, I can't blame her for the misunderstanding, but I can certainly blame the people who were advising her to keep her mail 'informal'. There is no context I know of in which anonymous messages are regarded as courteous or proper, or even as acceptable, and email is no exception. Being informal does not mean tossing common courtesy out the window. Anonymous messages are not 'informal': they are childish and offensive, even when they are carried by electrons. We will discuss this point further in chapter 2.

Some business firms instruct their employees that business emails should be prepared with the same care as business letters. You probably don't need to devote that level of attention to your emails, but, when in doubt, you should always err on the side of caution. More time, care and attention is better than less, and more editing and proofreading is better than less.

1.3 WHAT THIS BOOK DOES NOT COVER

First, this book does not attempt to deal with technical questions. If you have a technical question about your email, you should consult your manual, look at your online Help files, or talk to your technical support staff. There are also quite a few books which deal with the technical side of email, though some of these are advanced works aimed at technically sophisticated readers.

I will be assuming that you have a mailer program up and running, and that you have enough technical knowledge to send emails. (If this puzzles you, see the beginning of chapter 2.) I will also be assuming that you have a few basic computing skills, such as the ability to perform cut-and-paste operations (moving or copying text from one place to another).

Second, I am not trying to give you advice about very informal emails sent to close friends, colleagues and fellow enthusiasts. Emails sent in these circumstances are typically much more relaxed than emails written to strangers. They may contain all sorts of jokes, slang expressions and cute little doodahs; they may consist of incomplete sentences, and they often receive little or no proofreading and editing. Here is an example:

Caught the latest Spielberg flick last nite. Wow and
Wow and >>**WOW!!!**<< Havent had my head
feasted like that since our old pal Luke shot down his
last imperail baddy. The special fx are just TREMEN-
JOUS!!! :^0 :^0

   - - N

Depending on your tastes, you may or may not
consider this a suitable way of mailing a close friend.
But I will leave that decision to you. This book deals
only with emails to strangers, and with business emails
in general.

1.4 THE WORST MISTAKE YOU CAN MAKE

In comparison with most other kinds of writing, emails
are typically hasty. But, when you are writing a serious
email to a stranger, you must resist the temptation to
do it hastily.

Many people, when they are composing an email,
think to themselves, 'If I can save myself a little time
and effort here, that'll be a good idea.' It is not a good
idea: in fact, it is a *terrible* idea. When you are writing
a serious email, absolutely the *last* thing you should be
trying to do is to save yourself a little time.

What you should be trying to do instead is to *make
life easy for the people you are mailing*. After all, you
are the one who is approaching somebody else for
assistance. Therefore it is your responsibility to do
everything you can to ensure that giving you that assistance is as easy as it can be for the other people.

And saving your own time won't achieve this. You

can save your own time by making your message so hasty and so badly written that your recipients can hardly understand what you're talking about. This forces them to do a good deal of unnecessary work just in order to figure out what it is you want. In other words, saving your own time is irresponsible, childish and offensive. On top of all this, it is ineffective: many recipients simply won't bother to respond at all to a badly written message. Or – as we will see later in this book – recipients may be genuinely unable to understand what you're talking about.

If you have obviously spent no more than twenty seconds in composing your message, do you really think that the person at the other end is going to spend ten or fifteen minutes writing a careful reply? If you think that, then you have a serious problem with reality.

The single most important thing to understand about writing successful emails is this: *good emails take time and effort to write.* A good email simply cannot be thrown together hastily and then fired off. Unless you have a Mozart-like gift for getting everything perfect at the first attempt – and, let's face it: you don't – you must be prepared to spend some time in thinking about your message, in writing it, in editing and polishing it, and finally in proofreading it, before you let it go.

1.5 SOME THINGS TO KEEP IN MIND

No matter how you send your email, you are using somebody else's equipment. Possibly you are sending your mail from a computer which belongs to your employer, or to your university, or to an Internet café. Even if you own your computer, you are surely paying someone to connect you to the Internet, which means that you are using their equipment. And, in any case, your messages will be travelling along wires that belong to somebody else, and via a series of other people's computers, before they reach their destinations.

Consequently, a lot of other people have a stake in your mail messages, and these people have a right to demand that you use their equipment in a manner which is legal, responsible and honourable. If you fail to meet these not-very-demanding conditions, you will probably find that those other people are no longer willing to allow you to use their equipment, and you may find yourself banned from sending any emails at all.

Note in particular that you may not send personal emails from your computer at work without the permission of your employer. Ignoring this very reasonable requirement may cost you your job, especially if you send a personal email which offends somebody.

Email is cheaper than paper mail, or 'snail mail', as it is often known, but it is not free. Somebody has to pay for every mail that is sent. As a rule of thumb, the cost of an email is divided about equally between the sender and the receiver. If you are not the one who signs the cheques for your email, remember that somebody else is coughing up the money to keep you in business, and try not to spend that money foolishly. And, of course, bear in mind that your mails are costing your recipients money. This is one reason why electronic junk mail is so infuriating.

Remember that your recipient is a human being whose language, culture and humour may be very different from yours. Be very careful with slang expressions, with idioms, with jokes, and with appeals to the details of your culture. What is currently trendy in your circle may be utterly incomprehensible to readers elsewhere, especially among those whose first language is not English, but not only there.

For example, we in Britain have recently been reading about a popular television presenter who was caught with a prostitute, and this revelation has led to a flurry of jokes about that presenter and prostitutes. Many of us find these jokes very funny, but they will be meaningless to anyone outside Britain who hasn't heard about the story, and they may be highly offensive to readers in some societies where prostitution is not considered a fit subject for jokes.

Above all, be very careful with sarcasm. Sarcastic remarks can easily be badly misunderstood, and they may produce unintended but nevertheless great offence.

Among less emotive topics, observe that measurements do not travel well. You may be comfortable with square miles and degrees Fahrenheit, but these units will be so much Greek to many of your readers, who are only used to square kilometres and degrees Celsius. And date formats can also be a problem. To an American, 11/6 means November 6th, while, to most of the rest of the world, it means 11 June.

In all cases, it is *your* responsibility to see to it that your recipients are not confused, bewildered or offended by your email messages.

There is another point. I can hardly believe I need to mention this, but colleagues assure me that there are people out there who don't seem to understand it. Remember that the earth is divided into twenty-four time zones, and that local time varies greatly from one place to another. So, if you are wondering why you haven't yet had a reply to the obviously fascinating and brilliant email you sent some ago, it may be that the reason is merely that it is the middle of the night where your recipient lives, and he is sound asleep.

Finally, bear this fact in mind: once you click on the Send button on your mailer, your email is gone. All the king's horses and all the king's men can't bring it back again, and neither can all the computer technicians in the world. If you've made a mistake, then you are doomed: all of your recipients will shortly be reading your blundering words. And almost every one of us has had the grim experience of clicking on that button and then realizing, moments later, 'Oh, no! I made a big mistake!' You can keep these awful moments to a minimum if you make a habit of checking and double-checking and triple-checking your messages before you send them. Sure, this takes time, but trying to clean up after your mistakes takes time, too, and it's a lot more unpleasant.

(An aside: one or two mailer programs contain a button called 'Recall this message'. This is meant to give you the chance to pull back a message about which you suddenly develop second thoughts. But this button very seldom works, even if you click on it only ten seconds later, and it never works after a minute or two. If your mailer has this thing, just forget about it. Get your message right before you send it.)

1.6 SOME NO-NOS OF EMAIL

There are a number of badly mistaken beliefs and attitudes which are depressingly widespread among inexperienced users of email. Here is a summary of some of the most familiar ones.

1. It's a good idea to save time in writing emails.
2. I need a response right away.
3. Look how witty/clever/important I am.
4. I need to express my personality.
5. I'm going to give you a piece of my mind.
6. I'm not really dealing with a human being here.
7. Everybody's familiar with my language and my culture.
8. Everybody enjoys my sense of humour.
9. Everybody uses the same computer and the same software that I use.
10. Everybody remembers every word of my emails.
11. Everybody is healthy and has perfect eyesight.
12. Email doesn't cost anything.
13. Email is confidential.
14. Email is not subject to the laws covering other communications.

I've already touched upon a couple of these blunders. In the rest of the book, we'll be looking at almost all of them in some detail.

1.7 A REMINDER

Read this passage and remember it, always, when you are mailing strangers.

The people you are mailing are *busy*. They have jobs and lives to look after, and they don't have much time for dealing with emails from strangers. They are courteous, and they will try to be helpful, but only if your behaviour demonstrates that you deserve a helpful response.

Nobody is going to devote more time and trouble to a reply than you have devoted to writing your email in the first place. If your message is hasty and sloppy, and has obviously been dashed off in only a few seconds, then nobody is going to spend more than a few seconds in constructing a reply – and very many people won't bother to reply at all.

If you want your recipients to devote some time and effort to replying to your message, then you must show them you deserve this by devoting time and effort to your own message.

You must write your message as clearly, as carefully and as explicitly as you can. You must write it in the very best standard English you can muster, and you must edit it and polish it until you can't see any more short-comings. You must learn the courtesies and conventions of email – which are not very different from the courtesies and conventions of other kinds of writing.

Email is no excuse for haste, sloppiness, rudeness or any kind of childish or irresponsible behaviour. And email is no place to display your personality or your eccentric beliefs.

Finally, an email is a document, and it must not be treated lightly merely because it's not inscribed on a piece of paper. A promise made by email is still a promise. And an offensive remark in an email is still offensive.

> *Chapter summary:*
>
> • A business email must be composed in a businesslike manner

2
Getting Started with Email

2.1 WHAT YOU NEED

If you already have your email up and running, you can probably skip this section. But, if you haven't sent an email yet, you need to know a few things.

The first thing you need, of course, is a computer. But a computer won't send or receive email until it's equipped with a few accessories.

The most urgent requirement is a **mailer program**, or **mailer** for short. A mailer is a piece of software which is designed to allow the sending and receiving of electronic mail. There are many mailers on the market, and new ones appear with some regularity, as do updated versions of older mailers.

If you are using a computer which you don't own – at work, at your university, or in an Internet café – then the machine will be equipped with a mailer selected by somebody else, and you won't have much choice in the matter. Your home computer doubtless arrived with a mailer program already included, or 'bundled', in the jargon. But be aware that you don't have to use that mailer. If you find you don't like it, you can go out and buy another mailer and install that on your computer. You can even have two or three mailers sitting on your machine, and choose among them according to your mood. Providing you are using only one email address, each mailer will allow you to read all your mail.

There are certain features which are provided by almost every mailer on the market. We will be talking about some of these features at suitable places in the book. But here's a small warning: when I tell you that practically every mailer in existence has a certain feature, it is just possible that your mailer lacks that feature. I'll try to draw attention to this possibility whenever I can, but I have not used every mailer on the market, and even I may sometimes be surprised by the shortcomings of particular mailers. If you discover that your mailer lacks a useful feature which practically all mailers have, this might be a good reason to buy a new mailer.

But the mailer still won't do anything until you are connected to the Internet. Your work machine will have that connection already provided. On your home computer, however, you will have to arrange the connection yourself – and doing this will cost money. For this purpose you need to sign an agreement with a business firm which provides Internet connections. Such a firm is an **Internet service provider**, or **ISP**.

There exist many ISPs. Some of them are giant multinational businesses, while others are small local firms, but they all provide much the same service. Quite possibly your home computer arrived with an offer from an ISP to provide you with service. If you like, you can simply accept the offer by following the instructions provided. But you don't have to do this. There will be other ISPs operating in your area, and you might be wise to talk to some of your more experienced friends about their experience of prices and quality of service.

(Note that an ISP does not merely provide email. It provides a full suite of Internet services, including the ability to search the World Wide Web for information and to read pages that you find interesting, the ability to make your own web pages available to the world, and many other things.)

The next thing you need is an **email address**. This is the address which everybody else must use when sending you mail. Your address is unique to you: it distinguishes you from every other person on the Internet. The second part of your address is determined by your provider, but you have some freedom in choosing the first part, your username. See the next section for advice on making this choice.

There remains one more thing: a physical connection to the wires through which Internet links run, allowing you to go **on line**. There are two ways of arranging this.

One way is to use a **modem**, a device which allows you to make the connection through an ordinary telephone line. These days, almost every computer comes with a modem built in, and all you have to do is to buy a suitably long modem cable from your local computer shop, plug one end into the place provided on your computer, and plug the other end into a phone jack on the wall (after unplugging the phone that was there). This will give you the required connection, but note that your phones will not work while your computer is on line, unless you have a second phone line put in just to service your computer.

The other way is to have a permanent wire built in to your house or other establishment. This is the normal procedure with computers in business and at universities. It was not formerly usual for home computers, but it is now becoming more frequent, thanks to the growing availability of **broadband** connections in private houses. A broadband connection offers much faster service for all Internet purposes than do modems and traditional wires. Broadband services are typically offered by television cable companies and telephone companies, but at present they are not available everywhere, and you will have to check to see if they are available in your area.

This is all you need to send and receive email. But, in order to gain full benefit from your connection to the Internet, you will need a **browser**, a program which allows you to read web pages. Your home computer has undoubtedly come equipped with a browser built in; popular browsers are Netscape Navigator and Internet Explorer, but others exist, and you can always buy a new one (or perhaps download one for free from the Web). Another tool you will need is a **search engine**, a piece of software which allows you to search the World Wide Web for pages on particular topics. There are a number of search engines; among the popular ones are Google, Yahoo!, AltaVista and Ask Jeeves. Your browser probably makes one or more of these readily available; in any case, they are free.

These programs are enormously valuable, but they are irrelevant to email, except in one circumstance: you can use a browser in order to send and receive mail on a newsgroup, as explained in section 9.10.

2.2 CHOOSING A USERNAME

Your email address consists of two parts. The part after the at-sign (@) is the **domain name**, the name of the email system to which you are subscribed, and this is the same for everybody on that system. For your computer at home, this is the name of your Internet service provider, the company which connects you to the Internet and to which you are probably paying a monthly fee. The part before the at-sign is your **username**, the part that distinguishes you from every other person on that system.

Now, your provider will allow you some freedom in choosing your username, but there are limits imposed by every ISP, and you will not be offered a completely free choice. Ideally, your username should be as similar as possible to your name. Suppose your name is Katie Garner. Then you would probably like to have an address that looks something like this:

Katie.Garner@whiz.net

This looks professional and serious. And it has clear advantages. Look at your **inbox**, or mail spool, the list of emails you have received and not yet deleted. You will see that the sender of each email is identified in some way, probably by username. And having your emails flagged Katie.Garner is desirable. That way, your friends will recognize your messages instantly, while the strangers you have mailed will realize at once that you are probably a real person sending a real message, and not just one more infuriating purveyor of junk mail.

Some providers will make you settle for something like this:

kmgarner22@whiz.net

This format is not nearly as good as the first one, but it's just about acceptable, since your name is still visible, if now much less prominent. But some providers will lumber you with an algebraic username like this:

kmg18ff73@whiz.net

And this is not acceptable. Now your identity is buried in a crowd of cryptic characters, and your name is not visible at all. This is bad, for several reasons. One reason is this. Like everybody who is electronically active, I get loads of electronic junk mail, or **spam**, as it is commonly called. And very many of those junk mails arrive flagged with algebraic usernames of exactly this kind. Now, like every experienced user of email, I skip through my mail in the morning, deleting all the junk mails without bothering to open them. If your emails arrive looking like this, there is a grave danger that they will be mistaken for junk and instantly deleted – especially if you have failed to provide a good subject line, as explained in the next chapter.

Moreover, usernames consisting of strings of meaningless characters are hard to remember and hard to
type accurately. Katie's friends will have little trouble
remembering Katie.Garner or typing it correctly, but
something like kmg18ff73 will be a chore for them to
recall and a headache to type correctly.

So, if your provider insists on lumbering you with
a dreadful username like this, I suggest you look for
another provider, one which is more obliging.

Note that it is essential to include your surname
in your username. Suppose you don't, and opt for
something like this:

Katie@whiz.net

Now the consequence will be that, for many of your
recipients, your emails will wind up flagged like this:

Katie

Why is this bad? First, it is childish to use your first
name alone, as we will see further in the section on
signatures. Second, I get lots and lots of emails from
people who sign themselves just 'Katie' or 'Samantha'
or the like, and all of them are junk. These are the
people who are trying to sell me mortgages, or Viagra,
or investment opportunities, or pornography. Naturally, when I see a message from Katie or Samantha, I
delete it instantly. Do you want your emails to be
deleted instantly?

Some people use their surnames alone as usernames.
But this can be a little misleading if your surname

happens to be 'Dennis' or 'Malcolm', since such names can easily be taken as first names.

Finally, you must resist the temptation to choose a cutesy username like RadRapper or hotfloozie or elf-maiden. Usernames like these are typically chosen by fourteen-year-olds, and they are fine if you never expect to mail anybody but close friends. But the rest of the world, on seeing a username like this, will very likely conclude that you still have a lot of growing up to do, and that you are not a person to be taken seriously. Can you really imagine mailing a bank about a possible job and signing yourself hotfloozie? If you already have one of these things, it's time to get rid of it and choose something more professional-looking.

2.3 TYPEFACES AND LINE LENGTH

Your mailer doubtless comes equipped with a default typeface. This will be a plain font, in black, probably twelve-point. Unless you discover a problem with your default setting, you should leave it alone.

You should *not* try to fool around with fancy fonts. If you change your mailer's setting to some cutesy font, or if you change its colour to red or green or purple, then I've got news for you: out of every hundred people who receive your emails, one hundred people will be annoyed or disgusted, and zero people will be impressed. And readers who are colour-blind may be unable to read your mail at all. Oh, and don't change the background colour. Anybody who receives an email in white lettering on a fluorescent purple background is going to close his eyes and delete the awful mess at once.

Even worse is changing the size of your type. The standard twelve-point type is just about big enough to be readable by a recipient with average eyesight. If you change to a smaller typeface, then there is a great danger that many recipients will be unable to read your messages. Even eleven-point type, the default selected by a few mailers, is uncomfortably small for many people. Not everybody has perfect eyesight, and some people suffer from very poor eyesight, but they still need to use email. You should not use a typeface smaller than twelve-point.

I get mail fairly regularly from two or three people who seem to have set their mailers to use what looks like eight-point type. Their messages are completely unreadable on my screen. If I badly want to read their mails, I have to engage in some tedious and time-consuming manipulation in order to convert their texts into something that I can read. You will not be surprised to hear that I seldom want to read their contributions that badly. Unreadable messages are an excellent reason for reaching for the Delete button.

Remember one of the no-nos from chapter 1: email is no place to express your personality. If your personality requires fancy purple letters, save them for your bedroom wall. Stick to businesslike fonts for business purposes.

It is wise to check the line length used by your mailer. This is easy to do. Just start writing an email (which you are not going to send), and type until the text wraps – that is, until the text starts a new line. Then count the characters on one complete line, *including the spaces*. The total should not be greater than seventy, and some experienced commentators recommend a maximum of sixty-five characters.

If your lines are too long, then I'm afraid you must consult your manual, or your on-line Help function, and find out how to shorten the lines (you will probably find your line length given under **preferences**). Otherwise, your emails are going to look like this on many people's screens:

The American cereal maize, or sweet corn, reached the Basque
Country in the 16th century. It proved to be better adapted
to Basque conditions than the traditional wheat and millet – both
more productive and more reliable. Within a century maize had become
the staple crop, and the periodic famines which had once forced
the people to eat acorns were a thing of the past.

This kind of thing is annoyingly hard to read, and no one will thank you for filling his screen with it. (But I am told that some mailers don't allow you to alter the line length. If yours doesn't, and you find yourself stuck with an awkward length, this is an excellent excuse for buying a new mailer.)

2.4 SIGNATURE

Would you write a business letter and send it off without putting your name at the end? I hope not. But very many people commit this very blunder with every email they send: they fail to sign their messages.

Failure to sign your emails is thoughtless, rude and just plain dumb. Sending unsigned messages is one of the quickest ways of convincing your recipients that you are a backward child. True, your username *may* contain your name, but then again it may not. In any case, ordinary etiquette on the Net, just as anywhere else, requires a signature at the end of a message.

You may prefer to use a formal version of your name:

Katherine M. Garner

Or you may prefer an everyday version:

Katie Garner

Or, if you don't mind concealing your sex, you may even prefer to use your initials:

K. M. Garner

All of these are fine, and the choice among them is purely a matter of taste. But note that initials are used far more often by men than by women, and as a result many readers will instantly assume that 'K. M. Garner' is a man.

But note carefully: you *must* sign your full name, including your surname. It is completely unacceptable to sign yourself with your first name alone:

Katie

Small children identify themselves by their first names only, but grown-ups do not. When you are mailing people you don't know, signing with your first name alone is childish. Don't do it. Use your full name.

There is a further problem if you are commonly known as 'Pat' or as 'Sandy'. Names like these can be conferred upon both sexes, and so, if you sign yourself Pat Richards or Sandy McCarver, recipients will be unable to guess your sex, and some of them may jump to the wrong conclusion. If you think you might find this embarrassing, then you should consider a more formal version, such as 'Patrick' or 'Patricia', or 'Alexander' or 'Sandra'. Signing yourself Christine (Chris) Woods is awkward but effective: now everybody can see that you are a woman named 'Christine' who prefers to be known as 'Chris'.

You don't have to type out your name every time you send mail. Somewhere in your mailer program, probably in the section labelled **preferences**, is an option called **signature**, or perhaps **.sig**. If you haven't already discovered the signature option, look for it now.

The signature option allows you to type in the signature of your choice. Once you have done this, your chosen signature will automatically be attached to the end of every email you send. As you are typing your message, you can usually see your signature, so you know it is there. And, of course, you can edit that signature, if you want to. If you are mailing a close friend, you might prefer to delete your ordinary signature and to replace it with something more informal. (I'm told that a few mailers fail to display your signature. If you have one of these, this is a good excuse to buy a new mailer.)

Even better, some mailers allow you to compose two signatures – say, a formal one and an informal one – and to choose which one you want every time you write an email. And a few mailers will compose and insert your signature automatically, with no action from you, though I can't guarantee that you will be pleased by the result.

There is one more important advantage to using a signature, quite apart from ordinary courtesy. The technology of email is not infallible, and occasionally an email message arrives at its destination with its last part missing. Now, if your recipient can see your signature at the end of your mail, then he knows that the entire message has arrived safely. But, if all he sees is some lines of text followed abruptly by a blank space, then he has no way of being sure that he has received the whole message. As always, it is your job to make life easy for the people you are mailing.

While you're in the signature option, it's an excellent idea to add your email address after your name. This practice is universally considered to be courteous and professional. Moreover, as we will see later in the book, some mailers have the bad habit of stripping from the beginning of an email all information about the source of that mail. Therefore, your signature, with your email address, might provide the *only* way for readers to know who you are and how to mail you. So, your full signature might look like this:

Katherine M. Garner
Katie.Garner@whiz.net

For your private email at home, this is probably all you need. You don't want to publish your home address and home phone number, since the people who will be interested in this information will include your local burglars.

However, for your work email, you need to include a lot more. At work, you should include in your signature your name and your position and *all* of your contact details: the name of your employer, the employer's postal address (including the country: don't forget that), your email address, your phone number (in both domestic and international versions, if you do any business outside your country), your fax number (ditto), your mobile phone number (if you use that phone for business) and any other information that might help colleagues or customers to reach you. It is also good practice to include the URL (web address) of your web page or of your company's web page. So, at work, our friend Katie's email signature might look like this:

Katherine M. Garner
Commissioning Editor
Hobsbaum Publishers

22–24 Old London Road
Brighton
East Sussex BN1 7RR
UK

Katie.Garner@hobsbaum.co.uk

Tel: 01273–929292 (from UK); +44–1273–929292
(from abroad)
Fax: 01273–926457 (from UK); +44–1273–926457
(from abroad)
Mobile: 07799–834854

URL: http://www.hobsbaum.co.uk/html

This is what professionals do, and you should follow suit.

Some people like to decorate their private signatures with doodles or humorous quotations or pithy sayings. This is harmless enough, but I don't particularly recommend it. Doing this adds unnecessary length to every email you send, and unnecessary length is not an appealing property in an email. Moreover, if you mail the same people frequently, they will get tired of seeing your jokes or homilies over and over and over again. Anyway, your recipients have to *pay* for their email, and, the longer your message, the more they have to pay to receive it. (The dozen or so lines of Katie's business signature above are a different case: this information is *valuable*, and it is worth the space it occupies.)

It is also a bad idea to decorate your signature with a line of hyphens, or in fact a line of anything. You may think it looks nice, but there are blind or nearly blind people who have their email read aloud to them by their computers. Imagine the joy of sitting there while your machine intones 'hyphen, hyphen, hyphen, hyphen, hyphen, hyphen . . .' (My thanks to Kaitlin Duck Sherwood for pointing out this problem.)

And, of course, you *absolutely* must not include in your signature any expression of your political or religious beliefs. Such additions are offensive in the extreme, and they will get you banned from many electronic services. If you try this with your work email, you may find yourself in very serious trouble indeed. Save your political and religious beliefs for the contexts in which it is appropriate to express them.

2.5 SHARED ADDRESSES

Sometimes a couple share a single email address on their home computer. This arrangement saves a little money, but it can bring problems.

If the two people sharing the address are careless about signing their mail, then recipients may be genuinely confused about who is mailing them. Worse, a mail sent to one of the couple may be read by the other, and this can prove awkward. Even the most devoted couples like to keep a few secrets from each other. If Susie is arranging a surprise party for Mike's birthday, her plans will be spoiled if Mike happens to read an email meant for her.

Unless money is distressingly tight, you and your partner will probably be a lot more comfortable if you have your own individual addresses.

Chapter summary:

- Choose a professional-looking username
- Write in twelve-point black type on a white background
- Sign your emails with your full name

3
Starting a Message

3.1 DECIDING WHO TO MAIL

The heading of this section may look strange at first glance. Why would I want to offer you advice on who to mail? Surely you already know who you want to mail.

When you are sitting in front of your computer at home, this decision may indeed be easy. But things become much more complicated when you are at work or at university. The reason they become complicated is the existence of aliases.

An **alias** is a generic address for a group of people within an institution. An email sent to an alias will be sent to every person in the group covered by that alias. Consider my university, within which we have a large number of aliases. There is one alias for the academic staff in each department, another for all academic staff, another for administrative staff, another for technical support staff, another for the building maintenance staff, another for all staff, many more for picking out various groups of students, and so on. In addition, there are aliases which deal with particular functions rather than with groups of people, such as the one for social messages and the one for jokes; membership of these is voluntary.

Every institution containing a number of people has a comparable set of aliases. For example, a large publishing house might have aliases such as fiction, childrens, language and science for its various editorial divisions, plus editorial, publicity and finance for different groups of its staff, and perhaps social for social events. Aliases allow us to single out a particular group of people for an email without the wearisome necessity of typing out every single person's address. However, when aliases are available, it is important to choose an alias carefully.

The basic rule is this: mail as few people as possible. If your message is really only relevant to three people, then mail only those three. Don't send your message off to an alias which includes twenty or fifty or three hundred people. Clogging many people's inboxes with messages that they have no interest in is bad behaviour, and engaging in such behaviour will earn you no friends at all.

This advice is doubly important when you are complaining. If you have lost your swipe card, and your promised replacement is a week late in arriving, then take it up with the building supervisor whose responsibility it is. Don't complain loudly to everybody in the building. There is no need to embarrass the building supervisor in front of everybody, and doing so will merely convince your colleagues that you are an idiot. And, if it turns out that the supervisor's four-year-old daughter was rushed critically ill into hospital three days ago, your status as a colossal oaf will be abundantly confirmed.

Before you send an email to more than one person, think twice about whether they all need to see your mail.

Finally, there are times when you might think carefully about whether an email is a good idea at all. Email is more informal than many types of writing, but it is also a little detached and impersonal in comparison with direct contact. If you are passing on congratulations or commiserations, perhaps face-to-face conversation or even a phone call might be appreciated more than an email.

3.2 OVERDOING IT

You should not send an email without a good reason. Some people become so addicted to email that they can't leave it alone, and they sit at their desks for hours, firing off one email after another, more to entertain themselves than to get anything useful done. If you find yourself suffering from this problem, you must get a grip on yourself. Bombarding your colleagues or acquaintances with a stream of inconsequential emails is scarcely better than sending them junk mail. Your recipients will definitely not appreciate having their inboxes stuffed with endless messages from you, each one relaying a trivial bit of news or a joke or a scrap of gossip or your opinion of a new film.

Overdoing it in this way is a good way to lose friends. Before long, your emails will be welcome nowhere, and your more technically expert colleagues may take steps to block emails with your name attached. Then, of course, when you finally do have something important to say, nobody will bother to read it.

3.3 ADDRESS LINE AND CC LINES

When you open a window to send an email message, there will be several blank lines at the top of the window. The first of these is the address line.

The **address line** is the line into which you type the email address of the person you are mailing. I'm sure you already knew that, but I want to remind you here of the importance of checking and double-checking that address after you have typed it in. It is *extremely* easy to commit a typing error when you are typing in an address. It is doubly easy to make a mistake if the address is algebraic, containing a string of meaningless characters, or if it is unusually long, with several portions separated by dots, hyphens or twiddles. Suppose this is the address you are trying to type in:

khm27fjl82nt@jupiter.uni-muenchen.de

And suppose what you actually type is this:

khm27fj182nt@jupiter.uni-munchen.de

Is this right? No? Have you spotted the mistake? Feeling pretty good? Well, in fact, there are *two* mistakes in the second version. Did you catch both of them?

You probably spotted munchen for muenchen pretty

quickly. But did you catch 1 (the numeral one) in place of the required l (the small letter L)? These two characters are infuriatingly similar in appearance in many typefaces, and they get confused all the time. Much the same happens with the capital letter O and the numeral zero, which are likewise easily confused.

It is worth taking a few moments to check the address. Otherwise, you may find that your carefully crafted message **bounces**: that is, it simply comes straight back to you with an error message along the lines of 'no such address'. At this point you will *have* to do the proofreading which you neglected to do in the first place. Moreover, if you simply try to re-send the bounced mail to the right address, you will probably find that your mailer has decorated it with an irritating string of angle brackets, as explained in chapter 8. On top of this, your original subject line will have been erased and replaced with something like Error: message undeliverable. So you'll have to re-type the subject line.

On the whole, you will enjoy a more relaxed morning if you carefully proofread the address in the first place.

Even simple and familiar addresses can readily be mistyped. I mail my wife all the time, and I have her short and simple address in my head. Even so, one of my mails to her bounced on one occasion, because I had rattled off the familiar address and then plunged ahead without checking it – but I had made a simple typing error.

Addresses to which you frequently send mail can be stored in your mailer's **address book**, a facility which allows you to keep a list of a large number of addresses. There will be some simple way of choosing an address from the address book and of inserting it into the address line of a new message with a mere click of your mouse, with no typing required. If you haven't already discovered how to do this, take a look now.

It is possible to type two or more addresses onto the address line, but you must be careful about how you do this. On most mailers, the procedure is this: type in the first address, followed immediately by a comma, then a white space, and then the second address, and so on. Here is an example:

j.d.braun@violet.com, Sylvia.Korner@zeus.net, anr27dff11@plover.net

Once you leave the address line, your mailer will convert these into a neat list:

j.d.braun@violet.com
Sylvia.Korner@zeus.net
anr27dff11@plover.net

Below the address line is the **cc line**. This line provides the facility for sending copies of your message to people who you are not mailing directly. (The quaint abbreviation cc stands for 'carbon copy'; if you can remember carbon paper, you must be as old as I am.) You can type in additional addresses here, and your message will also be sent to those addresses.

Why the difference between the address line and the cc line? Well, the general idea is that the people on the cc line are simply being kept informed of what is going on, and they are not expected to do anything. Anybody from whom you are expecting a response should therefore appear on the address line, and not on the cc line.

The third line is the **bcc line**. The letters here stand for 'blind cc'. People whose addresses you type in here will also receive your message. However, while *all* your recipients will see all of the addresses on your address line and on your cc line, the addresses on the bcc line will be suppressed, and nobody will see them. The bcc line therefore provides a way of copying your message secretly to some recipients. In all my years of using email, I have never once found occasion to use the bcc line, but maybe you can think of a use for it.

3.4 SUBJECT LINES

When you send an email, there will be a line at the top of the window, somewhere just below the address to which you are sending your message, entitled *subject*. The words you type onto this line are the **subject line** for that message, and choosing a suitable subject line is a skill which separates competent emailers from ignorant bumblers.

When your message arrives in your recipient's in-box, the subject line you have provided will be displayed alongside your username. Look at the messages in your inbox, and you will see the subject lines chosen by the people who have mailed you.

Now, the first point is this: you *must* supply a subject line for each message. Leaving the subject line blank is appallingly ignorant and thoughtless. It is the subject line which tells the recipients what your message is about. If you don't provide a subject line, the recipients will have no clue what you are writing about, and they will be forced to open your mail and read it in order to find out even whether they have any interest in it. And not everybody is willing to do that. Some recipients will take this view: 'If he can't be bothered to tell me what this message is about, then I can't be bothered to read it.' And your message will be deleted without being read.

Moreover, the subject line you settle on must be *informative*. It is a waste of time to fill the subject line with useless words like Hi! or Information or Question. Such choices still give the recipients no clue as to what your message is about.

The problem of bad or absent subject lines becomes even worse when these are combined with bad or silly usernames, as described in the last chapter. Suppose that I come into work one morning and find the following new emails waiting for me in my inbox. Which ones do you think I will open, and which ones do you think I will simply delete at once? Bear in mind that, in real life, I typically get two hundred new messages every day, and not just nine. (Assume that I have recently sent a posting entitled No primitive languages to an electronic mailing list.)

1. Margaret.Rice Where can I buy your new book?
2. Samantha   hot farm girls
3. Sylvia
4. j.w.noble   Re: No primitive languages
5. Jason   Hello!
6. prettywoman   can you help me

   7. jgw24gg17h8   new invesment oppertunitys
   8. MRS ABACHA   URGENT
   9. Stan.Friedman   Request to write a chapter

Well, let's see. Number 1 is obviously a serious question, so I'll open it. Number 2 is junk mail: delete. Number 3 manages to violate just about every principle of good practice I have so far mentioned, and it will be quickly deleted. Number 4 is plainly a reply to my posting, so I'll read it. Numbers 5 and 6 are two more instances of bad behaviour, and they too will meet instant deletion. The illiterate number 7 is junk mail, so out it goes. Number 8 is a junk mail begging for money – I have received hundreds of these – so it too gets deleted. And number 9 is clearly a professional request, so I'll read that one.

These decisions were not too hard, were they? You should find little trouble in distinguishing the serious professional messages on the one hand from the junk mail and the childish fumblings on the other. When your email turns up in my inbox, which group will I assign it to?

The bad examples above illustrate a few more features of subject lines that deserve a mention. To start with, *do not* write your subject line all in capital letters, but *do* capitalize the first letter of the first word. We return to the subject of capital letters later in this chapter. Next, make sure your subject line is written in good English. The missing question mark in number 6, and the appalling illiteracy of number 7, are good examples of the sort of thing you should *not* be writing. Finally, do not include the word *urgent* in your subject line, unless your message really does urgently involve someone's life or security – or, in a strictly business context, a deadline. Writing *urgent* just to draw attention to yourself, or just to try to pressure your recipient, is an offence that ought to get you banned from the Internet.

Try to keep your subject line short – no more than six or seven words. Anything longer is pointless, because the excess will be chopped off when the subject line is displayed in your recipients' inboxes. The full subject line will be visible once your mail is opened, but meanwhile you have to persuade your recipients that they want to open it. Suppose you have chosen this as your subject line:

The recently agreed increase in Venezuelan crude-oil production

What many of your recipients will see in their inboxes is something like this:

The recently agreed increase in Venezuelan crud

The problem here is that the most important words have been left for the end, where they have been chopped. If you must use a long subject line, you should at least try to ensure that the first few words convey the general subject matter. Here is an improved version:

Venezuelan crude-oil production: the recently agreed increase

Now the worst that can happen in your readers' inboxes is this:

Venezuelan crude-oil production: the recently

And this, I hope you will agree, is an improvement.

I am not just joking here. Only the other day, I opened my inbox and saw this subject line staring at me:

Searching for some information about

And this, of course, was no help at all. The sender had wasted his subject line by filling it with useless words, leaving the essential words for the end, where they had been chopped because of the length limit.

Get the essential words in early, and avoid padding out the subject line with useless words. If you find this difficult, then spend a few minutes a day practising. And here is a handy rule of thumb: *never* put the word *information* into a subject line. This word is always a waste of space, space that could be used to explain what your message is about.

As it happens, when I opened the message whose subject line I've just been discussing, I found that the full subject line provided by the questioner was this:

Searching for some information about a certain article

This was, to say the least, disappointing. It seems that the sender just could not bring himself to say what he wanted in so many words – at least, not in his subject line. Instead, he resorted to vague, coy, roundabout words that never got the job done.

If your message is long, it is courteous to add the comment '[long]' to your subject line. For this purpose, 'long' is commonly understood as 'more than one hundred lines'. So, if you're writing two hundred lines on the Mittal affair (a recent political imbroglio in Britain), your subject line might look like this: The Mittal affair [long]. Doing so warns your readers that opening this message when they have only a few free moments is not a good idea.

If your message is a question, you should start the subject line with the sequence 'Q:'. This is explained in chapter 7, which deals with asking questions.

If your message is a request for action, then you would be wise to start the subject line with 'Req:'. An example:

Req: Open Day desk on Saturday

Even before they open this message, the recipients will realize that they are being asked to undertake some kind of action.

If your message is purely for information, and it requires no response of any kind from your recipients, then you should start the subject line with 'FYI:', which stands for 'for your information'. An example:

FYI: Open Day desk on Saturday

Now, in great contrast to the last message, this one makes it instantly clear to the recipients that they are simply being notified of what is going on, and that they are not being asked to do anything.

Do you see how helpful and considerate these conventions are? The thoughtful and skilful use of subject lines makes life very much easier for the people you mail. If you have trouble writing appropriate subject lines, then you should devote some time and effort to learning how to compose good ones. Your emails will be far more effective as a result.

You should *not* begin your subject line with 'Re:', which is Latin for 'about, concerning'. This item does not mean 'here is what my message is about'. It means 'I am replying to your mail with the following subject', and it is inserted automatically by your mailer when you reply to a message, as explained in chapter 8. Some junk mailers make a habit of attaching this 'Re:' to their junk mail, in the hope of persuading gullible recipients that the junk is a genuine reply. Experienced users of email are not deceived, and, if you make the mistake of writing 'Re:', your mail may be taken for junk and deleted at once.

There is one more special case. If your mail deals with a confidential matter, then it is *strongly* advisable to make this clear in the subject line. In most cases, I recommend using this word as the *entire* subject line:

Confidential

There is a good reason for this. Suppose you add a few words explaining what the confidential message is about:

Confidential: James Bannister

This may be slightly helpful to your recipient, but it has the unfortunate consequence that anyone who happens to walk past and glance at your recipient's screen may see this heading, and therefore realize at once that confidential messages are being exchanged about James Bannister. And this partly defeats the point of being confidential in the first place.

3.5 WRITING IN PLAINTEXT

Without exception, you should write your emails in **plaintext**. Plaintext is ordinary text, the kind you produce by using the characters on your keyboard, with no special keys like Command or Alt, and no other software at all.

This may seem blindingly obvious, but there are quite a few people out there who don't understand it. A couple of times a week, I receive emails which have been composed in HTML, the special markup language used for constructing web pages. An email in HTML looks like this:

```
<HTML><HEAD>
<TITLE></TITLE>
<STYLE type=text/css>TD {
   FONT-WEIGHT: normal; FONT-SIZE: 12px; FONT-
FAMILY: tahoma}
A:hover {
   COLOR: #0000ff}
```

And so on, for page after page.

Well, some fancy mailers can interpret HTML and

display the result in glorious Technicolor, but my
mailer can't, and all I see is lines and lines of meaningless HTML code. No doubt the text message is in there
somewhere, but the sender is a fool if he thinks I'm
going to wade through acres of gibberish to locate
some English words, and I delete every such message
at once – as do most people. Don't compose emails in
HTML unless you are certain that all your recipients
can deal with HTML messages.

Even worse, several times a week I get emails which
consist of nothing but gibberish from beginning to
end, like this example:

```
§&@'œ_•±ª7¬z>'A§F°§3_7æ|¶
*m~_^©™33@!±_=_/f\_··ª%iº7
```

And so on, perhaps for several pages. You get the
picture. Even the subject line looks like this.

It appears that the dim-witted senders have foolishly
composed these messes in the source code of a word
processor, or some other piece of software, and then
released them in this form. Very few mailers can cope
with this kind of thing, and you must be an idiot if
you think this is a good way of sending emails.

3.6 SALUTATION

In a letter, the **salutation** is the opening words, like
Dear Sir or *Dear Amanda*. Do you need a salutation in
an email, and, if so, what should it be?

There is probably no issue in email on which there
is so little agreed policy as here. No established con-

vention exists, and in practice usage varies enormously.

When you're mailing a friend, you are unlikely to have many problems in deciding how to address that friend. But mailing a stranger presents all kinds of complications.

To start with, you may not even know the sex of the person you are mailing. You may feel pretty confident about the sex of somebody named *Peter* or *Elizabeth*, or even of somebody from another country named *Sophia* or *Karl-Heinz*. But foreign names present all kinds of obstacles. For example, *Andrea* is a female name in English, but it's male in Italian. And *Jan* is female in English, but it's male in several other European languages.

Non-English names can be impossible to guess. What do you make of these personal names: Spanish *Pilar*, French *Odile*, Basque *Itziar*, Welsh *Iolyn*, Irish *Irial*, Hungarian *Imre*? The first three are female, the last three male. More complicated is the name *Inge*, which can be either male or female in Danish or in German, but which is strictly male in Swedish; the female form in Swedish is *Inga*. Moreover, names from most Asian and African languages are unlikely to reveal the sex of the owner to an English-speaker: Vietnamese *Phuong* or Japanese *Motoka*? (Both are female.)

Even English names can be treacherous. In the USA, the names *Vivian* and *Hilary* are strictly female, but in Britain they are sometimes conferred on men. In Britain, *Marion* is strictly female, but American bearers of the name have included Marion Morrison (better known as the tough-guy film actor John Wayne) and Marion Motley, one of the roughest, toughest

American football players of all time. We have sexually ambiguous names like *Chris* and *Sandy*. And not everybody realizes that the English name *Loreto* is female.

Just to complicate things still further, some peoples, such as the Hungarians, the Chinese and the Japanese, normally write their names surname first – though they may turn their names round when dealing with outsiders.

All this means that writing Dear Mr Mendizabal or Dear Ms Adler can be a risky business. And, as a further complication, there are women who dislike the title *Ms* and who insist on being known as *Mrs* or *Miss*. These women often make their preference clear in their email signatures, but, if you haven't yet seen their email signatures, this isn't much help.

If the person you are mailing is an academic, then you are probably safe in writing Dear Dr McCarthy, since almost every academic holds a doctorate. Less advisable is writing Dear Prof. Danvers. In the USA and Canada, and in other countries using the American system of academic ranks and nomenclature, almost every academic does indeed hold the title *Professor*. However, in Britain, in Europe, and in much of the rest of the world, very few academics hold the title *Professor*. In my experience, though, not many academics will take offence at either style, since at least it is clear that you are *trying* to be courteous.

What about throwing caution to the winds and addressing the other person by first name? Many people will tell you that email is an informal medium, and that quick use of first names is therefore acceptable. I am not so sure.

Americans are famous for shifting to first names almost instantly. But there are differences among Americans. California, for example, is famously laid back, while Boston and Philadelphia are altogether more buttoned-up.

Outside the States, English-speakers are often a little less quick to adopt first names. Britons are more cautious about using first names than are Americans, though they are much more relaxed about this now than they were thirty or forty years ago, when middle-class British men commonly addressed one another by surname alone, a practice which Americans find offensive.

Things can be very different in other languages. Addressing a German-speaker by his first name when he hasn't invited you to do so is a large faux pas. And addressing a speaker of Japanese by his first name in almost any circumstances at all is a grievous blunder. The rules for using names vary considerably from one society to another.

You might try something noncommittal, like *Good morning* or *Good afternoon*, but these are a bad idea, since you have no idea what time of day it will be locally when anybody reads your mail. Remember, when it's 10 a.m. in California, it's 6 p.m. in Britain, and it's dark in Asia. The even more noncommittal *Good day* sounds stiff to many Americans, though the Australian *G'day* is understood and accepted by almost all English-speakers as polite and friendly. But you can't use this if you're not Australian.

All this still doesn't answer the question we started with: what, if anything, should go into the salutation?

Well, I can't give you a definitive answer. The commonest way out is to use no salutation at all, and almost everybody considers this acceptable in emails. But, if omitting the salutation makes you uncomfortable, you are on your own. Do your best to come up with something polite, and keep your fingers crossed that you haven't misguessed your recipient's sex.

The exception is emails that are strictly business – for example, those sent by business firms to customers or suppliers. An email of this kind must have a salutation, and that salutation should be exactly what would appear if the message were being enclosed in a letter instead of an email.

3.7 SOME ELEMENTS OF COURTESY

If you are mailing a stranger, you must explain who you are and why you are mailing your recipient. This is no more than common courtesy. Email is no excuse for intruding upon somebody you don't know. Email gives you no right to demand somebody's attention, and still less to demand a response.

Regardless of who you are mailing, don't write anything you wouldn't say face to face. When you are sitting in front of your machine, it is easy to get the impression that other people are no more than remote disembodied abstractions. But, of course, they are real people, and careless emails can hurt their feelings just as much as a public dressing-down.

When you are making a request, write *please* or *could you*. Avoid writing *I need*, which sounds arrogant and supercilious.

3.8 WEBSITE EMAIL POP-UPS

Sometimes the owner of a website provides an email link. If you want to mail the owner, all you have to do is to click on the email address, and a little window will pop up on the screen for you to type your message into, with the address line already filled in.

This is perhaps convenient, but there are a couple of drawbacks. First, these pop-up windows are much narrower than ordinary email windows, and so your message will be squeezed into annoyingly short lines when it arrives. Second, since you are not using your own mailer, your signature will not be inserted automatically, and you will have to remember to type it in at the end of your message.

I find these drawbacks decidedly annoying. Consequently, I often just copy the recipient's email address into the address line of a new message on my own mailer, and then I go ahead just as I would with any other email. You can do the same if, like me, you are more comfortable using your own mailer.

> *Chapter summary:*
>
> - Double-check the address line
> - Write an informative subject line
> - Use 'Q', 'Req' and 'FYI' as appropriate, but never 'Re'
> - Write in plaintext

4

Presentation and Organization

4.1 USING GOOD ENGLISH

At this point I am probably going to make you nervous. In spite of what you may have been told about the informality of email, you should write your business emails in the best standard English you can muster. And I stress *standard* English.

Why do you need to write emails in standard English? There are several reasons, all of them good.

First, it is a blunt fact that quite a few people will interpret a poor command of standard English as a sign of low intelligence. This is not fair, of course, but it's the way things are. And it is not in your interest to give anybody the impression that you are an idiot.

Second, there are many more people who will simply be insulted by poor English, or even by typos. These people will react as follows: 'If he can't be bothered to make more effort than this, then I'm not going to waste my time on him.' Again, it is not going to help you to offend or annoy the people you are mailing, or to convince them that you do not deserve a reply.

Third, standard English is far more highly elaborated than any other variety of English. By this I mean that standard English has been developed in ways that will allow you to achieve any goal you may have in mind when dealing with strangers. Standard English provides the vocabulary and the structures to express anything you may want to express in a completely explicit manner.

Finally, standard English is agreed upon. There is an established set of conventions making up standard English: vocabulary, spelling, punctuation, grammar and word use. When we write in standard English, we can be reasonably confident that our readers will understand our meaning. The countless non-standard varieties of English around the globe differ greatly from one another, and departures from standard English are therefore far more likely to produce confusion and misunderstanding.

Matters are slightly complicated by the existence of two slightly different versions of standard English: the British standard and the American standard. The differences between these are not great, but they are very conspicuous, especially in spelling. You should, of course, try to stick to one version or the other, since mixing the two will please nobody.

If English is not your mother tongue, and you are worried that your imperfect English may produce a bad impression, then stop worrying. Practically nobody will mind if your non-native English is imperfect, so long as your messages are comprehensible.

It is native speakers of English who must be on their

mettle. Bad English from native speakers is what upsets so many readers.

It is beyond the scope of this book to offer detailed advice on how to write English well. If you need to work on your English, there are many useful books which you can consult. Two helpful Penguin books, both by R. L. Trask, are *Mind the Gaffe: The Penguin Guide to Common Errors in English* (for spelling, grammar and word use) and *The Penguin Guide to Punctuation*.

Here I will mention just a few basic points.

One: do *not* use 'simplified' spellings like *thru* for *through*, or *nite* for *night*. Such non-standard spellings will greatly annoy many readers, and they may puzzle readers who are not native speakers of English. Stick to standard spellings.

Two: do your best to use standard punctuation. Poor punctuation can make an email very hard to follow. And omitting punctuation altogether, as a few pathetic souls do, is grotesquely unacceptable.

Three: keep your punctuation under control. *Never* pile up exclamation marks: !!! Such messes look breathless and schoolgirlish, and they are entirely out of place in a serious email.

4.2 PARAGRAPHING

If your message is more than a few lines long, you should break it up into paragraphs, in such a way that each paragraph introduces a new point, however minor. And these paragraphs should be *short* – no more than seven or eight lines at the most.

Some people have trouble with this, and they produce enormous paragraphs that drag on for dozens of lines – fifty, sixty, seventy, eighty lines or more. Such huge paragraphs are bad in any kind of writing, but they are especially bad in emails. Why? Because the reader can see only a small part of the message at once, the part that fits into the window on the mailer. The absence of good paragraphing forces the reader to scroll through a long and dense mass of writing, trying to keep his place in the process, and possibly getting lost. No reader will thank you for this, and some readers will give up in exasperation.

If you suffer from the problem of endless paragraphs, then you will just have to take yourself in hand and force yourself to divide your text into short paragraphs. Otherwise, the outcome will be that readers' hearts will sink when they see your name in their inboxes, and their fingers will start twitching towards the Delete button.

You should put a blank line at the end of each paragraph – otherwise, the paragraphs will be jammed together densely, and much of the value of paragraphing will be lost. And you should *not* indent the first line of each paragraph. Indenting is normal in many other kinds of writing, but it doesn't travel well electronically, and it may cause havoc on your readers' screens. Don't indent.

4.3 FORMATTING

I assume that your typeface and your line length have been properly set, as explained in chapter 2. But there are some other points worth mentioning.

Do not hit the Return key (the carriage return) at the end of a line. The presence of carriage returns in your message may badly mess up the way it looks on your recipients' machines. Just keep typing, and let your mailer wrap (start a new line whenever required).

As far as possible, you should refrain from using the Tab key. Tabs and indents may look nice on your screen, but they don't travel well, and they may have the effect of scrambling your words on your recipients' screens.

This fact makes life difficult when you want to construct columns in your message. The ordinary way of making columns, of course, is to use the Tab key. But not all mailers will interpret the Tab commands as you intend, and the result on some screens may be chaos.

The other way of making columns is just to count out white spaces. This avoids the problems with the Tab key, but it runs into difficulties of its own. There are different kinds of typefaces – different, that is, in the way the characters are spaced out on the screen – and consequently your painstakingly aligned columns may disintegrate on your readers' screens.

So far as possible, it is best to avoid mailing columns. But I know there are times when columns are unavoidable. On these occasions, all you can do is to set up your columns in one way or the other and hope for the best.

Another thing you should stay away from is the special characters called control characters; these are discussed in some detail in chapter 5.

I turn now to a venerable question: should you type two blank spaces between sentences, or only one? In the days of manual typewriters, there was something of a convention among typists, particularly in the United States but not only there, that two white spaces should be typed between sentences. Many keyboard users today – including me – still automatically type those two white spaces. I type all my emails this way, and nobody has ever complained to me about a problem. But some experienced commentators report that typing two spaces can upset certain mailers, and they recommend typing only one white space between sentences.

I guess you should stick with whichever convention you are comfortable with, unless one of your recipients reports a problem.

On occasion, you may want to copy a portion of text from a document on your computer, perhaps a word-processed document, and to paste it into an email. If you do this, you *must* check the result. Quite often, this pasting process will wreck the formatting of the original, and the words that appear in your email will be scrambled into an unholy mess. If this happens, you must painstakingly clean up the mess, in order to produce something which is neat and easy to read. Leaving the mess in your mail is intolerably offensive.

Finally, if you have doubts about the appearance of your mail, you can check it by sending it first to yourself, in order to see what it looks like on a recipient's screen. Unfortunately, if you do this, and you then try to send the result to somebody else, you will probably find that your mailer has turned the whole message into a giant quotation, marked off by angle brackets, as explained in chapter 8.

4.4 GETTING TO THE POINT

Some people, when writing emails, find it very difficult to get to the point. These people burble on at length about this and that, filling up a chunk of screen, and then stop, without ever making it clear what they are expecting from the recipient.

Here is an example, directed at an editor in a publishing house:

> We in the Marketing Department have become concerned about Kozlowski's book. Sales of this book were healthy for four years, but in the last year they have dropped substantially. It may be that the book needs updating, or it may be that the recent partially similar book from Global is taking away sales. Certainly we cannot allow our book to remain on our list if sales continue to decline.

Now, what is the recipient supposed to do about this message? Urge the author to revise his book? Ask someone to examine the Global book and decide whether it is providing strong competition? Remove the book from the list? How can he tell? The message gives him no clue.

There is very little point in sending an email like

this one. Clearly the sender is hoping to get something done, but no reader can tell what that is. The sender should have spelled out exactly what is expected from the recipient. Here is an improved version:

> We in the Marketing Department have become concerned about Kozlowski's book. Sales of this book were healthy for four years, but in the last year they have dropped substantially. We cannot allow the book to remain on our list if sales continue to decline. Can we therefore ask you to do two things?
>
> 1. Ask a suitable person to look at the recent partially similar Global book and at Kozlowski's book and decide whether the problem is strong competition or the growing outdatedness of our book.
>
> 2. If outdatedness appears to be a problem, ask the author to revise his book urgently.
>
> If the problem proves to be nothing but competition, we'll have to consider our position later.

This version is effective: now the recipient knows exactly what is expected of him.

The best way to avoid sending such pointless emails is to plan ahead, to think carefully about what you are trying to achieve before you touch your keyboard.

4.5 ENUMERATION

Sometimes your email consists largely of a list of brief points. In this circumstance, you should consider presenting these points as an enumeration. An enumeration puts across what you have to say crisply, tersely and effectively. Here is an example:

The work on 'Proto-World', the hypothetical ancestor of all languages, is dismissed by linguists for the following reasons:

1. The method used is merely the accumulation of miscellaneous resemblances, a procedure which was dismissed as worthless by linguists over 200 years ago.

2. The authors make no attempt to explain what they count as a 'resemblance', and they rely solely on their own unsupported judgements.

3. In practice, their work shows that they are willing to accept anything at all as a 'resemblance', if it suits them to do so.

4. They show no awareness of the need to calculate a background score of resemblances arising wholly by chance, and to demonstrate that their data exceed chance by a significant margin.

5. On the rare occasion when they attempt any calculations at all, they invariably get those calculations horrendously wrong.

6. They decide in advance what conclusions they want to reach, and then they go trawling for scraps of evidence that appear to support those conclusions.

7. They present only the data that suit their purposes, and they silently suppress all contrary data.

8. The data which they do present are twisted, distorted and mangled almost out of recognition, in order to make them fit the required conclusions.

9. Some of their data do not exist at all, and have been fabricated by the authors.

10. They ignore or wave away the conclusions of erudite specialists based on generations of painstaking study.

If your message lends itself to presentation by enumeration, this choice can be highly effective in getting your thoughts across. Notice, though, that you need to leave a blank line after each point. Otherwise, the points will be scrunched together, and most of the effectiveness will be lost.

If you like, you can use bullet points instead of numbers. True bullet points (•) can't be transmitted by email, but you can use asterisks as a substitute. But, if you have more than two or three points, numbers are probably better, since numbers help readers to keep track of where they are.

Enumerations make life easier for your recipients. Those recipients can see at a glance how many points you are raising and just what those points are. They will find it easy to respond to individual points, and you in turn will immediately understand which responses belong to which points.

Especially when you are expecting your recipients to respond, use enumerations at every opportunity. Your recipients will thank you, and you will get more work done with less bother.

4.6 BREVITY

No email should be longer than it needs to be. Unnecessary length adds to the cost of sending and receiving a message, and it wastes the time of the recipients who have to wade through the mail.

Of course, some mail messages have to be long. However, if your message is long, try to summarize it in your first sentence or your first paragraph. Doing so makes life a good deal easier for your readers.

Long messages are especially likely to suffer from transmission glitches and thus to lose their final parts. Making sure that your signature appears at the end of your mail, as explained in chapter 2, will help your readers to know that they have received the whole message. But there is another and more explicit device. In a long message, you can type the word *END* at the end of the text, and tell your readers in your opening line that you have done so. If you do this, your readers will know for certain whether they have received the full message or not.

4.7 ABBREVIATIONS

I work in a department of Linguistics and English Language. When my colleagues and I email one another on departmental business, we commonly abbreviate *Linguistics* to *Lx* and *English Language* to *EL*. This is fine. After all, we use these words all the time, and using the abbreviated forms saves us some typing time. There is no difficulty about using the short forms, since everybody in the department is used to them and understands them at once.

But we don't use these abbreviations outside our department. When we need to mail anyone else in the university, we write the words out in full. We have to, because we can't be sure that anyone else will be able to understand our abbreviated forms. After all, *we* have no idea what short forms might be usual among the faculty in Art History or Chemistry, or among the staff in the finance office, and we wouldn't be pleased if these people dropped their incomprehensible abbreviations on us.

And this is something you should keep in mind when writing emails: don't use abbreviated forms. It's fine to use the short forms that are used by all speakers of English, like *Mr*, *a.m.*, *bc*, *FBI* and *UN*. And it's also acceptable to write *17th century* in place of *seventeenth century*, since there is no possibility that any reader will misunderstand the short form. But that's as far as it goes. Except when you are certain that an abbreviated form will be instantly understood by every person reading your mail, you must avoid short forms and write things out in full. And I advise against using the ampersand, &. Write out the word *and*.

It is *terrible* practice to write something like this in a public email:

> In reply to Jill Handley's comments on the evol hist of monogamy, I'd like to remind e/o that Markovich's comp modelling in the 1980s showed that monog behav would always emerge when the period of parental care of offspring exceeded 1 year.

Almost all readers will find this sort of thing irritating and distracting. And annoying your readers is too great a price to pay for the trivial benefit of saving seven seconds of writing.

There is another point. Countless thousands of the people who use email are not native speakers of English, and non-native speakers may have some difficulty in following abbreviated forms. Those people are doing you the huge courtesy of using your language, English. You can afford to burn seven seconds on the return courtesy of writing emails that are as clear as possible.

There is a particular kind of abbreviation which has become unpleasantly frequent in some quarters. I'm talking about things like *IMHO* for 'in my humble opinion' and *AFAIK* for 'as far as I know'. Some people have somehow acquired the notion that inserting these things into emails is good practice. Not so: this is a very bad idea. Why?

First, the sentiment expressed by the words 'in my humble opinion' is false modesty. If you think your view is valuable enough to announce electronically, perhaps all over the world, then you do not truly believe that your opinion is 'humble', and you should not pretend otherwise.

Second, the expression is pointless. If you are expressing your opinion, then, unless your writing is so bad that your message is incomprehensible, anybody with half a brain can see that you are expressing your opinion. Typing extra material in order to *tell* your readers that you are giving your opinion is therefore a gross waste of time. So, by typing *IMHO*, you have not saved any time: you have merely wasted your time. And the same goes for the elaborated version *IMNSHO*, which means 'in my not-so-humble opinion'.

I can't raise the same objection to *AFAIK*. Unlike *IMHO*, this one genuinely has some content. But I've just tested my own slow and inept typing, and it took me a grand total of four seconds to type out *as far as I know* in full. Is your time *really* so scarce and valuable that saving four seconds in typing an email is more important than ensuring that all your readers will understand you at once? Are you really certain that everybody in the world will understand *AFAIK* anyway?

The same goes for *OTOH* 'on the other hand', *BTW* 'by the way', *RSN* 'real soon now', *TIA* 'thanks in advance', *IWBNI* 'it would be nice if', and many others in this vein. Most of these will be understood by readers who have years of experience with email, and you are probably safe in using them with friends who have such experience, but they should be avoided in mailing strangers.

Even an experienced user may at times be flummoxed by one of these creations. The abbreviation *YMMV* is an American creation; many Americans understand it, but Net-users outside the States may be baffled by it. The force of it is 'I don't guarantee that this will work the way I have described it', and the letters stand for 'your mileage may vary', a disclaimer commonly heard in American TV commercials for cars.

Stay away from these toys. Saving a few seconds of your time is less important than ensuring that you are clearly understood. And tossing these things into your mail just to demonstrate that you are au fait with them is childish.

Finally, I have just recently begun seeing emails like this one for the first time:

I need 2 find some work on women's speech 4 an SA I am riting. R U aware of any work set in Britain?

This is an example of the style used in text messaging with mobile phones. Now, if I described this as 'unacceptable' in emails, I would hardly be doing justice to the truth. Writing emails in such a way is unspeakably ghastly. Anybody who sees this kind of mess in his inbox is probably going to decide at once that the sender is an imbecile. *Don't do it*. This is even worse than writing in capital letters, the subject of my next section.

4.8 CAPITAL LETTERS

Astonishingly frequent are emails written entirely in capital letters. I get several of these every week. Here is a typical example:

> I WOULD LIKE TO KNOW MORE ABOUT LEARNING A
> SECOND LANGUAGE AND THE SOURCES OF MOTIVATION
> THAT CAN HELP A NEW LEARNER CARRY ON IS
> THE TEACHER PART OF THE MOTIVATION, THE
> ENVIRONMENT . . .

This example has many other problems: almost no punctuation, sentences run together, second sentence incomplete. But the big problem is those capital letters.

First, as anybody will tell you, capital letters are the electronic equivalent of screaming. You must therefore never write in capital letters, since this practice is considered intolerably rude by everybody on the Internet.

On top of this, though, writing in capital letters is unspeakably childish. Small children learn to write in capital letters first, and only later do they learn the small letters. If you write in capital letters, you will give everybody the impression that you are an idiot child who has not yet learned the small letters – or at least that you are an idiot who has not yet noticed that the rest of the world writes in mixed capital and small letters.

Writing in capital letters is one of the dumbest mistakes you can make. Don't do it. There is no excuse for it. (Possible exception: see below.)

On the other hand, it is essential to write the capital

letters which are required by the ordinary rules of
English orthography: at the beginning of each sentence,
and at the beginning of names and certain other words.
Writing something like this will impress nobody:

> i can't agree with richard elliot's analysis of french
> verb phrases. the analysis looks superficially elegant,
> but that elegance is achieved, i believe, only by
> stretching anne-marie dupont's well-known generaliz-
> ation further than it was ever meant to go.

Why do people write in this bizarre way? Are they too
lazy to use the Shift key? Have they not *discovered* the
Shift key? Are they so slow-witted that they have never
noticed that nobody writes English in this way?

Recently I received a mail written like this, and I
asked the sender why she was doing it. She replied that
she had been told that using capital letters in email
was rude! Well, there's a lesson here. The people who
warned her against capital letters no doubt believed
that they were making themselves entirely clear – and
yet their advice was badly misinterpreted. This is a
sobering reminder of just how easy it is for us to
misunderstand one another's words, and a reminder
therefore of the importance of making every effort to
produce emails that are as clear and as unambiguous
as they can possibly be.

There is another possibility, of course. Perhaps you
write without capital letters because you have your
own individual ideas about how English should be
written, and you are eager to let everyone know how
excellent your ideas are. Well, if so, I've got news

for you: nobody is interested. Readers will only be interested, if at all, in what you have to say, and saying it in such an eccentric way will only annoy those readers and distract their attention from the content of your message. Forget it. Remember: email is not the place to express your personality. And it is also not the place to shove down every reader's throat your opinions about subjects that are of no relevance to your content.

Exception: There is just one conceivable special case which can justify writing either entirely in capital letters or entirely in small letters. That occurs when you are disabled, and you have trouble using the Shift key. In such a circumstance, you may find it more or less essential to avoid using the Shift key, and so you may be forced to write in capitals or without capitals. This is completely understandable, but how will anyone know? You can simply tell people, of course, but perhaps you would rather not announce your disability to the world. In this case, I can only suggest that you use the Caps-lock key as a replacement for the Shift key. This is cumbersome, but it works.

4.9 STYLE

No aspect of writing is harder to teach than good style, and I'm not going to try to give you lessons in style here. Nevertheless, I can usefully draw attention to a few common failings which you should try to avoid.

The first is pomposity. In my experience, this is not a particularly common failing in emails, since most poor emailers err on the side of excessive casualness, not on the side of excessive stuffiness. But every now and again I see a message like this one:

> I am doing some research on the history of Spanish, but I'm having trouble finding any information. Can you suggest some good places to look?

The problem here is this. The questioner plainly knows nothing at all about the history of Spanish, and he doesn't even know where to look to find out something about this topic. Yet he assures us solemnly that he is *doing research*. But writing an essay on a topic you initially know nothing about is not what most of us understand by the term *research*. The questioner is therefore being pointlessly pompous.

He should have written something like this:

> I'm trying to find out something about the history of Spanish . . .

or

> I've been asked to write an essay on the history of Spanish . . .

As always, keep your writing plain, direct and simple. Don't put on airs, and don't pretend to be grander than you are.

One of the on-line guides to email which I consulted while preparing this book, one which is in most respects excellent, astonishingly advises you to use big words when you want to impress recipients with your importance. This is dreadful advice. Foolishly tossing around a few big words may allow you to impress the odd dimwit, but most people who read the result will draw the conclusion – probably the correct conclusion – that you are a pompous idiot. Don't try it.

I sometimes get emails from some of the most eminent and distinguished scholars in my field. All of these people write in a plain, unaffected style. They say what they have to say, and they never try to impress the rest of us with their importance. You should follow their example.

The second failing is the opposite: breeziness. You will impress no one by writing like this:

Hi, guys!!! Gotta little poser for ya here. Seems the latest gene map of our boring old continent Europe shrieks about a big link between our beret-wearing Basque pals and those chilly northern reindeer-herders the Lapps. How ya gonna 'splain *that*?

Fortunately, the emailers who suffer from this disease are not numerous, and I don't see this kind of thing more than once or twice a year.

Far more common than pomposity or breeziness is wordiness. Wordiness is a bad habit which is much encouraged by bureaucratic paperwork. Many people whose working lives consist largely of dealing with paperwork find that they can't break the habit of using six flabby words where one simple word will do, even in emails and even in conversation. Here are a few examples of what I mean:

Bad	*Good*
on a daily basis	every day
on a regular basis	regularly *or* all the time
at this moment in time	now *or* at present
in an emergency situation	in an emergency
prior to initiation of employment	before starting work

If you suffer from this problem, you would do well to find a little time to practise writing plain English. Your colleagues will thank you for it, since no one enjoys wading through globs of such glutinous English.

4.10 VULGARITY

It should hardly be necessary to warn you against using vulgar or obscene words in public emails. Even the milder vulgarities are wholly out of place in a message sent to a stranger, even when they are clearly intended as jokes and marked as jokes in the manner described in chapter 5.

There are just two circumstances in which the use of vulgar words is permissible in a serious email: first, when you need to quote a passage containing these words, and, second, when these words themselves are your subject.

Now, in these circumstances, the use of vulgar words is usually beyond objection, and, in ordinary writing, it would be normal to write the offending words out in full. With email, however, there is a peculiar complication, and you might be well advised to replace these words with coy substitutes like f**k and s**t.

The problem is this. Some people, and some organizations, in an attempt to block out junk mail advertising pornography, have installed filtering devices on their computers. These filters are technologically crude, and all they can do at present is to search incoming mail for particular sequences of letters, and to reject any mail containing a prohibited sequence. And this can be a nuisance.

Some time ago, a colleague asked publicly for comments on a new web page he had just posted. I responded with a few comments, and I was startled to receive a stern message telling me that my message had been rejected by his computer.

By chance, I ran into him several weeks later, and I told him about the rejection. He explained to me that he had installed one of these filters on his machine – and I work at the University of Sussex. His filter had decided that 'Sussex' was a naughty word, and blocked my mail.

A few years ago, there was a kerfuffle when the citizens of the English town of Scunthorpe discovered that their emails were being blocked all over the place. I have never heard whether somebody managed to fix this problem, but you can see the difficulties.

4.11 MISUSE OF THE SUBJECT LINE

The purpose of the subject line is to tell your recipients what your message is about before they open it. Bear in mind that the subject line is *not* part of the text of your message. Treating the subject line as part of your text is bad behaviour. Look at this bad example:

[subject line] Colour photocopier

I need to copy an article from _Scientific American_.
Can anybody tell me where I can find one?

Most readers will be flummoxed by this. Below is the proper way of asking this question:

[subject line] Looking for a colour photocopier

I need to copy an article from _Scientific American_.
Can anybody tell me where I can find a colour photocopier?

No one will struggle with this.

4.12 EDITING AND POLISHING

Once you have finished writing your message, it is time to edit it and proofread it. And I mean this very seriously.

If you are merely mailing a colleague to say Ready for lunch when you are, there is plainly no point in editing and polishing your message. This message can hardly be misunderstood, and the odd typo will cause no harm.

But serious emails to strangers are a very different matter. Now it is of the greatest importance to make a good impression and to be as clear and accurate as possible. So, you must read through your message slowly and carefully, looking for typos and correcting them, and looking also for misstatements, errors of fact, instances of ambiguous wording, and anything else that might interfere with your message.

Countless people do not understand this. They routinely dash off a piece of mail and then fire it off without any editing or proofreading at all. The result in most cases is a message containing a couple of gross typos, and very often also a message which is difficult to understand.

Failure to proofread your mail is an expression of contempt for your recipients. If you fail to proofread, then in effect you are saying this: 'You are so insignificant that it's not even worth the bother of proofreading messages to you.' Now, is this the impression you want to give when you approach a stranger? And do you think your recipients will be pleased at this open display of your attitude?

As always, courtesy in email is not very different from courtesy in other domains. If you can't be bothered to undertake even the minimal courtesy of checking your message before you send it, then you are demonstrating to the whole world that you are a backward child who has yet to grasp even the most obvious conventions of proper behaviour.

But it's not merely courtesy that's at issue. An uncorrected typo can have a devastating effect on your message. Take me. I have a curious habit of omitting the word *not* when I am typing. So, not infrequently, I find on proofreading that I have typed this:

You must send anonymous messages.

when I mean this:

> You must not send anonymous messages.

You can see how catastrophic such a typo can be. Even though you may not suffer from my problem, you are hardly likely to be an impeccable typist, and all kinds of damaging errors may creep into your typing. And just one typo can ruin your message so completely that the message becomes worthless.

There exist all sorts of electronic props to help you with your writing: spellcheckers, grammar checkers, style checkers. Assuming you can get these programs to run on your email, you may find them of some use in catching a few blatant errors – though running a style checker on an email is overkill, and not recommended.

But a spellchecker is no substitute for good spelling. It can catch some mistakes, but all it can really do is to check whether the word on the screen exists in its dictionary. It has no way of knowing whether the word that is there is the word that's *supposed* to be there. So it won't pick up such common errors as *not* for *now*, *there* for *their*, *he* for *the*, *were* for *where*, and countless others. Moreover, a spellchecker will not catch an omitted word, like my omitted *not* above. You can spellcheck all you like, but you must still proofread your message carefully before you send it.

Quite apart from catching errors, reading through your text may reveal other shortcomings. You may decide that one sentence is ambiguous and misleading. You may find that you have accidentally said something which is wrong. You may even discover that you have failed to mention an important point that you had planned to include.

These are not hypothetical possibilities, remote from the real world. Every week I receive emails from strangers which are error-ridden, obscure, hard to follow and on occasion completely incomprehensible. Failure to edit is a common shortcoming, and I am privileged to see the awful consequences. Later in this book we'll be looking at some genuine examples.

Remember: once you have sent your message, it's gone, and nobody can pull it back. All your blunders will be staring out from the inboxes of your recipients. A little time devoted to editing can save you a great deal of embarrassment.

But how much time should you devote to editing your message? I am not suggesting that you should painstakingly wade through your text eight or ten times, replacing a word here, inserting a comma there, and generally polishing your words until they glisten. After all, an email is not an entry in a prize essay competition, and the search for perfect prose is best left for other contexts.

Nevertheless, you need to strike a balance between editing and time. Obsessive polishing is out of place, but failure to edit at all is even worse. Learn to check your mail before you send it.

4.13 FLAMING

The sending of angry and abusive email is called **flaming**, and nobody likes flaming. Most of us get upset once in a while when we read our email, but most of us manage to avoid flaming. Here is a valuable piece of advice:

> *Never send an email in anger.*

If you find yourself upset by something you find in your inbox, *don't* fire off an instant reply. There is a large probability that you will quickly come to regret that hasty reply. Most people who indulge in flaming regret their outburst before very long.

So, if you're upset, then wait a while before replying. Wait until you've cooled down. Wait till the next day. If possible, wait until you can see the funny side of it.

Your reputation is at stake here. Even one thoughtless outburst may quickly earn you a reputation as a foul-mouthed troublemaker, and you may discover that your emails are no longer welcome in some quarters.

There is a custom in some circles of tolerating a brief outburst of flaming providing it is conspicuously marked off as such, like this:

FLAME ON

In my view, McAlister's ideas are so much cretinous sludge.

FLAME OFF

I suppose this practice is at least better than an uncontrolled outburst of abuse. But I can't really endorse it. In emails to strangers, it is far better to refrain from flaming at all.

Chapter summary:

- Write in your best standard English
- Use short paragraphs separated by blank lines
- Plan ahead
- Use enumerations where possible
- Be brief, but not cryptic
- Use capital letters normally
- Edit and proofread your messages
- Don't flame

5
Making It
Look Nice

5.1 SPECIAL CHARACTERS

There are ninety-four characters which appear on
every English-language computer keyboard. These include the twenty-six small letters, the twenty-six capital
letters, the ten digits, the punctuation marks, four
kinds of brackets, and the characters @ $ % ^ & * + =
| / \ ~ _ , plus one more that I'll mention shortly.
These ninety-four, plus the space, are the **ASCII
characters** (the word is pronounced ASK-ee, with the
'cat' vowel). Each one of these ninety-five characters is
produced by hitting one of the ordinary typewriter
keys on your keyboard, possibly with the shift key.
And each one is expressed electronically by an internationally standard code which is universally used and
understood. In fact, the total number of ASCII codes
is 128, but the other thirty-three are used for purposes
other than encoding characters. Since computers
always start counting with zero, the ASCII codes run
from 0 to 127.

Every mailer program on every computer in the

English-speaking world can handle these ninety-five characters without difficulty, with the exception of that one character I haven't mentioned yet. The exception is ASCII code number 35. On an American keyboard, number 35 represents the hash mark, #. But British keyboards are different. Since the ASCII code was invented in the United States (its name stands for 'American Standard Code for Information Interchange'), it contains the American dollar sign, $, but not the British pound sign, £, or any other currency symbol. British manufacturers have found it convenient to make room for the pound sign on British keyboards, which means that one of the other symbols has to be removed. The character that has been bounced is the hash mark, and so code number 35 represents the pound sign on a British keyboard.

If you have the £ on your keyboard, and you type it into an email, it will show up as £ on another British machine but as # on all other machines. Likewise, if you have # on your keyboard, it will show up variously as # or as £ on other people's machines. This is the only case in which the ASCII code may fail to reproduce your typing faithfully. As a consequence, a sequence like #500 has long been understood as being equivalent to £500 in email, and in fact the hash mark is itself sometimes called the 'pound sign'.

Currency can be a nuisance. But what about all the other useful characters and symbols that we sometimes like to use? Well, the technical experts have for years now been promising us software that can handle everything from the International Phonetic Alphabet to Chinese characters. This software is based on a system called **Unicode**, and the idea is that all software on all machines will one day work with Unicode. Sadly, though, such software is still rather scarce, and mailers are feebler than most programs at coping with unusual characters.

These days, however, most *computers* (not mailers) can produce and display a sizeable range of additional characters, such as § ¶ ß © æ. These extra characters are called **control characters**, since they are typically produced by combining an ordinary keystroke with one of the control keys, which have names like Control, Command and Alt. Note, though, that some keyboards carry a couple of these on plain-looking keys. For example, my keyboard has § and ±, which are nevertheless not ASCII characters. And these characters are electronically encoded by an additional 128 code numbers, 128 to 255, known as **extended ASCII**.

Now, you may discover that your mailer program can display at least some of these additional characters, and you may therefore be tempted to decorate your emails with them. I have just one word of advice: *don't*.

The problem is that most mailers cannot display these special characters. So, if you include some of them in your emails, your recipients will see nothing but mysterious coded sequences like =E38 in place of your pretty characters, and the result will be unintelligible.

Just to make things worse, the control characters are encoded differently on Macs and on PCs. Thus, even if you and your friend both have machines and mailers that can display these characters, if one of you has a Mac and the other a PC, things are not going to work.

So, sad as it may seem when your machine can produce all these wonderful characters, you must avoid using them in your emails, and stick resolutely to the ninety-five ordinary plain vanilla ASCII characters. If you need to express the other things, you will have to write them out in English words.

Just to close this section, there is a convention of writing USD (for 'US dollars') in place of $ and UKP (for 'UK pounds') in place of £, whenever you anticipate possible difficulties. These versions are always understood.

5.2 DIACRITICS

Diacritics, informally called 'accents', are the little dots and squiggles sometimes added to printed letters to indicate something about their pronunciation. In English, we make little use of these things, except in a few names, like *Zoë* and *Brontë*, and in words and phrases of foreign origin, like *café*, *façade*, *Gemütlichkeit*, *mañana* and *bête noire*. Most other European languages, however, make heavy use of diacritics, and there are times when we want to write words or names from these languages. What can we do?

These days, many mailers can produce and display at least a few of the more familiar diacritics, such as *é*, *ü*, *ñ* and *ç*. If your mailer can do this, great – but you can't assume that the people you are mailing will also have such talented mailers.

If your mailer can produce these things, but your recipient's mailer can't display them, then your recipient is going to see macaroni wherever you have typed a diacritic. For example, your typed mañana might appear as mae4%ana, and your Schröder might show up as Schrq&;7der. This is what happens, and you can see the problem: many of these will be more or less incomprehensible.

There are three ways of addressing this problem, but not one of them is wholly satisfactory.

Solution one is to ignore the diacritics altogether. Write façade as facade, Schröder as Schroder (or as Schroeder, which in fact is perfectly acceptable in German), mañana as manana, and so on. With a little goodwill, your readers will be able to follow all of these, and in practice this is the solution which is most widely used.

Very occasionally, though, this solution can come a cropper in an embarrassing way. Take Turkish. The Turkish alphabet, uniquely, makes use of both an ordinary dotted *i* and an entirely distinct dotless *ı*. As it happens, the Turkish word *sık* is harmless and means only 'thick', while the word *sik* is obscene.

Solution two is to represent the diacritics with following keystrokes. In this approach, mañana is written as man~ana, déjà vu as de'ja' vu, tschüss as tschu"s, détente as de'tente, and so on. This is a little cumbersome, but at least it preserves the information carried by the diacritics. However, this solution will not work with some diacritics, because there are no suitable characters on the keyboard for representing them.

Solution three is available only if your mailer can produce diacritics, and it's really only convenient if you're using no more than one or two diacritics. Suppose I'm writing an email in which I really need to make crucial use of the n-tilde, ñ. My mailer can produce this, but I know that it will show up as macaroni on some other people's mailers. What I can do is this. At the beginning of my message, I type the following:

> I'm using the n-tilde, which on your mailer looks like this: ñ.

Now, all of my recipients whose mailers can display the n-tilde will see exactly this. But the other people will see something like this:

> I'm using the n-tilde, which on your mailer looks like this: e4%.

These readers will now know that, when the sequence ie4%or appears on their screens, they should interpret it as iñor (this happens to be the Basque word for 'anybody').

5.3 SUPERSCRIPTS AND SUBSCRIPTS

Mailers cannot display superscripts or subscripts. With superscripts, there is a conventional way of representing them on screen, using the character ^, which is on your keyboard. If, for example, you need to write x^2, you can express this in email as x^2. Everybody will understand this device.

For subscripts, unfortunately, there is no comparable convention. So, if you want to write the chemical formula for alcohol, CH_3CH_2OH, the best you can do is to write CH3CH2OH.

5.4 EMPHASIS

Most mailers cannot handle *italics*, **boldface** or <u>underlining</u>. This can be a nuisance, since sometimes we want to emphasize a word or a phrase.

In order to mark emphasis, a convention has grown up of setting off the material to be emphasized between a pair of asterisks. Here is an example:

> Relatedness between languages is not demonstrated by compiling lists of miscellaneous resemblances, and indeed relatedness *cannot* be shown in such a way.

Here the asterisks show that the word *cannot* is meant to be strongly stressed. In printing, we might use italics or boldface for this purpose, but with email the asterisks are the best we can do.

This convention is not yet universal, and some people prefer other ways of marking emphasis, but the asterisks are both the most widely used convention and the most satisfactory one, and I recommend their use.

Another fairly widely used device is reversed angle brackets:

> . . . relatedness >cannot< be shown in such a way.

I don't like this device as much: I think it's not as easy on the eye as asterisks. But, if you prefer it, you'll be in good company.

One further point. In a serious email, you should *not* pile up asterisks or anything else in order to mark emphasis. Things like the following are poor practice:

```
. . . relatedness ***cannot*** be shown in such a way.
. . . relatedness >>>cannot<<< be shown in such a way.
```

Such exaggerated emphasis looks schoolgirlish, and it should be avoided.

You might wonder why we don't simply resort to capital letters for emphasis. Why can't I simply write this?

```
. . . relatedness CANNOT be shown in such a way.
```

Well, many people do write this. But not everybody likes it. As we saw in chapter 4, capital letters are the electronic equivalent of shouting, and some readers will consider you rude if you resort to capital letters. On the whole, it is safer and wiser to stick to the asterisks.

5.5 TITLES

In ordinary writing, the title of a large work, such as a book or a film, is written in italics: *The Brothers Karamazov*, *Raiders of the Lost Ark*. Since italics are not available in email, we need a substitute. The most widely used convention is to enclose such a title within a pair of underscores: _The Brothers Karamazov_, _Raiders of the Lost Ark_.

The title of a small work, such as a poem or an essay, is conventionally enclosed within single quotes: 'An Irish airman foresees his death', 'A modest proposal'. There is no difficulty about doing the same in an email: 'An Irish airman foresees his death', 'A modest proposal'.

Note also that we capitalize every significant word in the title of a large work, but it is not necessary to do so in the title of a small work.

5.6 WRITING ABOUT WORDS AND NAMES

In my own profession of linguistics, we need constantly to write about words. But almost everybody has occasion to write about words once in a while. In ordinary print, there are conventions for doing this, which you should learn and follow, but these conventions are a little awkward to transfer into email.

When, in ordinary writing, you need to name an English word which you are talking about, you have two choices: you can either cite the word in italics, or you can enclose it in single quotation marks (not double quotes). So, in ordinary writing, either of the following is acceptable:

The words *champagne* and *campaign* have the same origin.

The words 'champagne' and 'campaign' have the same origin.

However, in ordinary writing, when you want to name a word from a language other than English, you *must* cite it in italics. In many cases, you will want to provide a brief English translation, or *gloss*, and this is done by writing the English gloss immediately after the word, enclosed in single quotes, with no other punctuation:

The words 'champagne' and 'campaign' both derive from Latin *campania* 'open country'.

This is easy and straightforward. But how do we do this inside an email? Single quotes are no problem, of course, but a mailer can't produce italics. So we need a substitute.

In this context, the most widely used substitute for italics is a pair of angle brackets, like these: < >. Using this convention, my last example looks like this:

The words 'champagne' and 'campaign' both derive from Latin <campania> 'open country'.

Here the angle brackets set off the foreign word in a way that is visually striking but still easy on the eye. This is the convention I recommend.

There is just one possible difficulty with this convention. Some exceptionally fancy mailers have a problem with angle brackets, which they interpret as marking instructions for displaying messages. If your recipients complain about this, then you may have to find another solution, such as setting off the foreign material with a pair of asterisks, in the fashion recommended above for marking emphasis. But, in all my years of sending emails about language, I have only once bumped into somebody whose mailer complained about my angle brackets. So I don't think you need to worry very much.

By the way, if you're wondering why you need to bother to mark words which you are talking about, the reason is that failure to do so can confuse your reader badly. Take a look at these two examples:

The word processor came into use about 1910.
The word 'processor' came into use about 1910.

The second statement is true, while the first is wrong by about seventy years. As always, it is your responsibility to ensure that what you have written is clear and unambiguous.

Names, like words, require special treatment if we are to avoid obscurity and absurdity. One of the novels on my bookshelf carries the following surprising statement about the author:

Susanna Gregory is a pseudonym.

This is a preposterous thing to say about Ms Gregory: she may be many things, but she is assuredly not a pseudonym. What the writer *should* have written, of course, is this:

'Susanna Gregory' is a pseudonym.

Here the single quotes show that what the writer is talking about is the *name* and not the woman. Names, like words, must be enclosed within single quotes when we write about them, and you should follow this convention in your email:

'Susanna Gregory' is a pseudonym.

5.7 EMOTICONS

Emoticons are the cute little sideways faces produced with keystrokes from your keyboard. They are meant to suggest something about the writer's mental state, as with :-(for 'I'm unhappy' and :^0 for 'I'm surprised'.

Emoticons – the name means 'emotional icons' – are used because they can be produced, and for no better reason. There is no problem with using these things when you are mailing close friends, if you like, though overusing them will quickly make your writing tiresome. However, with just a single exception, emoticons have absolutely no place in serious emails, and you should not use them.

The single exception is this one: ;-), commonly known as the **smiley**. By universal agreement, this doodah means 'I'm joking', and it is typed at the end of a sentence which is meant to be a joke. Here is an example:

> Mr Hansen's new book argues that English was introduced to Britain, not by the Anglo-Saxons, as the conventional view would have it, but by the Vikings who conquered England in 1016. Historians will, of course, be eager to learn about this scholarly breakthrough. ;-)

The point here is that the writer is being sarcastic. Hansen is plainly a crackpot, and the force of the writer's sarcastic words is that historians will want to steer clear of this drivel.

Why do we bother with the smiley? There is a good reason. When we are speaking, our tone of voice and our expression give it away quickly that we are joking. But, in writing, including in emails, these clues are lost. There is therefore a danger that our joking words will be taken seriously by some readers. The smiley is there to ensure that this mistake does not happen.

Many regular users of email will tell you that marking your jokes with smileys is good practice, and I agree. It is surprisingly easy to write something which in your eyes is an obvious joke but which some readers will nevertheless take seriously, possibly resulting in the taking of offence. Careful use of the smiley will prevent this.

But there is another point about the smiley which people will rarely tell you, but which is essential for you to understand. The smiley is not a neutral piece of punctuation, like a comma or a semicolon. The smiley accompanies a joke, and so it can only be properly used when it is proper to make jokes in the first place.

Making jokes in your email is a sign of *solidarity*. If I make a joke, I am implying the following: 'I regard myself as a member of your group, and therefore I consider that I have the right to make jokes.'

Take me. I am a professional linguist, and I regard myself as a member of the community of professional linguists. When I mail my professional colleagues, either individually or collectively, I do not hesitate to make a joke if I think a joke is appropriate, and of course I mark my jokes with smileys. But I don't do this often: I doubt that I use a smiley more often than once a month. I do not see myself as the Groucho Marx of my profession, and joking is hardly the point of my professional emails.

But, when solidarity is absent, then joking is entirely out of place, and so is the smiley. Again, if you are mailing a bank about a possible job, then jokes are out of order. Using the smiley is a little bit like slapping someone on the back, and treating potential employers like bosom buddies is a horrendous gaffe.

There is another point. Don't assume that a smiley will wash away all sins. If your words are offensive, then they are no less offensive because a smiley follows. The presence of a smiley does not make your words or your views any cuddlier than they would be with no smiley.

5.8 CITING URLS AND EMAIL ADDRESSES

Sometimes you may want to cite a URL, the address of a web page. Now, every URL begins with the sequence http://, and as a result there is a common convention of omitting this material when citing a URL – for example, on your business card. If the URL of your personal web page is http://www.whiz.net/kmg/index.html, then you might cite this merely as www.whiz.net/kmg/index.html in most circumstances.

However, when you cite a URL in an email, it is a good idea to cite the whole thing, including the http://. The reason for this is that many mailers today can spot a URL inside an email message and automatically convert it into a live link, so that anyone reading the email need only click on the URL in order to go directly to the web page. This is a great convenience for readers. But quite a few mailers achieve this by looking for that initial sequence http://. So, if this sequence is missing, those mailers will fail to create a live link.

When you cite a URL, you must not put a full stop at the end. It is a very bad idea to write something like this:

My URL is http://www.whiz.net/kmg/index.html.

Perhaps you have already spotted the problem. It now looks as though that final full stop is part of the URL. Consequently, when a recipient's mailer tries to create a live link, it will include that full stop, which should not be there, and the link won't work. And a reader who tries merely to copy the URL into his search engine will also very likely type in that full stop, and again he won't get through. This kind of needless problem can lead to bad-tempered exchanges.

There are two ways of dealing with this problem. First, you can type a space at the end of the URL, before the full stop:

My URL is http://www.whiz.net/kmg/index.html .

This may look a bit funny, but it should avoid the problem.

Second, you can make a policy of putting a URL on a line by itself, with no punctuation:

My URL is

> http://www.whiz.net/kmg/index.html

Now the full stop has vanished altogether. This may trouble stylistic purists, but it guarantees that no mailer and no reader can misread the URL.

Occasionally a URL is so long that it won't fit onto a single line:

The URL you want is

> http://uni-muenchen.de/linguistik/
> h.-j.bollenbacher/~typologie/data/europ/
> nomina.html

In my experience, there is nothing to be done about this. Mailers which try to convert this string into a live link will fail. Even human beings may be bewildered and fail to grasp what they are looking at. About the only thing I can suggest is enclosing the whole thing within a pair of angle brackets:

The URL you want is

> <http://uni-muenchen.de/linguistik/
> h.-j.bollenbacher/~typologie/data/europ/
> nomina.html>

The mailers will probably still fail, but at least human readers will now probably see what is going on, so that they can copy the right material into their search engines.

Similar problems may arise in citing an email address, and the same solutions are available. It is again a bad idea to write this:

Katie's email is Katie.Garner@whiz.net.

Sophisticated readers will know that an email address never ends in a full stop, but you can't safely assume that all your readers are that sophisticated. So, type a space:

Katie's email is Katie.Garner@whiz.net .

Or use a separate line:

Katie's email is
    Katie.Garner@whiz.net

As always, a few seconds of thought and care on your part can save your readers a great deal of grief.

(But bear one thing in mind: you must not pass on somebody's email address without permission. See section 10.1.)

5.9 TYPING INSTRUCTIONS

Sometimes you may find it necessary to mail somebody instructions for doing something on a keyboard, and in this case you will need to tell your correspondent exactly which keys to hit. This calls for a little care.

Unfortunately, there is as yet no universal set of conventions for doing this, and several notations are in use.

The name of a key which is not a character key always gets an initial capital letter: Shift, Return, Control, and so on. Some people write these names entirely in capitals (SHIFT, RETURN, CONTROL), but this is hardly necessary. Some people enclose these names in quotation marks, while others use square brackets or even angle brackets: Hit 'Return' or Hit [Return] or Hit <Return>.

Whichever convention you adopt, the key point is to make sure that you enclose nothing but the material to be typed. If you write Hit 'Return.' in your email, then you are instructing your reader to hit first the Return key and then the full stop, which is not what you intend. American readers should particularly note this, since standard American punctuation – unlike standard British punctuation – requires full stops and other final punctuation marks to be placed inside quotation marks, even when they logically don't belong there. Write Hit 'Return'.

If your instructions require the reader to hold down one of the control keys while hitting another key, then the usual practice is to name the control key first, followed by a plus sign and then the name of the other key. So, if you want your reader to hold down the Alt key and hit the character 8, then you write this: Type 'Alt + 8'. If your reader needs to hold down *two* control keys, write it like this: Type 'Shift + Alt + 3'.

A complication can arise here when one of the control keys to be pressed is the Shift key. The problem is that not every keyboard puts all the characters in the same place. For example, on my keyboard the question mark (?) is on the same key as the slash (/), and it is the question mark which requires the Shift key to be pressed. But you might find that the question mark is somewhere else on your keyboard, perhaps sharing a key with some other character – let's say the equal sign (=) – while the slash might be sharing a key with the at-sign (@).

In this circumstance, if I want you to hit Alt plus ?, then, if I write Type 'Shift + Alt + /', you are going to get the wrong result. The solution, of course, is to write this instead: Type 'Alt + ?'. But now your reader must be alert enough to note that producing the question mark requires the unmentioned Shift key.

5.10 ASIDES

Some people like to decorate their emails with asides, little editorial comments expressing the writer's attitude. There are far too many of these to list here, and everybody is free to create new ones at will. Among the common ones are <hollow laughter> to express cynicism or disillusionment, <hug> to express gratitude, <yawn> to express boredom, <pleading look> to reinforce a request, <eg> ('evil grin') to express smug satisfaction, and [LOL] ('laughing out loud') or [ROTFL] ('rolling on the floor laughing') to express amusement at what the other person has written.

These things are fine in personal emails, but they are wholly out of place in business emails. They suffer from the same problem as smileys: their use expresses solidarity, and solidarity cannot be assumed in mailing strangers. And the abbreviated ones, of course, may be unintelligible to some readers.

Chapter summary:

- Stick to ASCII characters
- Be cautious with diacritics
- Use a pair of asterisks for emphasis
- Set off English words with single quotes
- Set off foreign words with angle brackets
- Be careful about presenting email addresses, URLs and typing instructions

---

6
Attachments

6.1 SENDING ATTACHMENTS

An **attachment** is a copy of a document which is already sitting on your computer, and which you tack onto an email, so that it arrives at the other end along with your email. In principle, you can attach a document of any kind – even a photograph – so long as you already have it on your computer.

In business emails, the most frequent attachments are documents which have been prepared with specialist software like word processors or spreadsheets. In private emails, photographs and other kinds of pictures are probably the most usual attachments.

These days, almost every mailer provides some simple way of attaching documents to emails. If you haven't already learned to do this, you are well advised to find out. But don't get carried away. As we will see shortly, attachments present certain difficulties, and you should not try to send an attachment unless you have a good reason. In fact, you will be well advised to *avoid* sending attachments. Sending attachments just because your machine can send them is a foolish waste of time, and worse than that. Let's see why.

6.2 COMPATIBILITY

Mailers are compatible. An email sent from one mailer can be received and read on any other mailer in the world – providing the message is written in plaintext and avoids diacritics and special characters. But attachments are a very different matter.

Attachments are created, or placed on your computer, by using some suitable piece of software. And not all software is the same.

If your computer is a Mac, then you probably use Mac software. But, if your computer is a PC, then you probably use Microsoft software. And here there is a familiar problem: Mac software and Microsoft software are not compatible. In other words, a document prepared with one kind of software cannot be opened or read with the other kind of software. This is just as true of attachments as it is of anything else. So, if you send an attachment to somebody who uses a different kind of computer from yours, it is highly likely that the recipient will be unable to open your attachment. And sending an attachment which cannot be opened is an utter waste of time for all concerned.

It's even worse than this. Even if your recipients use the same kind of machine as you, they may not have installed all of the flashy software that you have on your machine. So, if you attach a document which you have created by using some gee-whiz piece of fancy software, your recipients may still be unable to open your document, because they don't have the right software. Even if they have the same software in principle, your document composed in HotWire version 9.0 probably can't be opened by your friends who are using version 8.6.

This is why you should keep your attachments to a minimum. If you must send an attachment, keep it simple. Use only the plainest and most familiar software for creating attachments, and refrain from using anything fancy. The fancier your software, the greater the likelihood that the people at the other end won't be able to open your attachments.

In fact, before you send an attachment to anybody, it is wise to check with your intended recipients, in order to find out whether they are likely to be able to read your document. Doing so is courteous and thoughtful, and it is a sign of a professional attitude.

However, if you just fire off an attachment without checking, assuming that everybody in the world uses the same computer as you and the same software as you, then you are . . . well, I was tempted to use another word, but let's just say you are a little dozy.

When you do send an attachment, it is very good practice to explain in the accompanying email exactly what software is required to open the attachment. Some clever mailers can figure this out for themselves, but not all can, and it is thoughtless and offensive to leave your hapless recipients to fumble about with one piece of software after another, trying to figure out what is required.

One final point. There are still some mailer programs in use which cannot handle attachments at all.

If you try to send an attachment to somebody who is using one of these mailers, all he will get is pages and pages and pages of gibberish.

6.3 CONVERSIONS

There are various ways of dealing with the compatibility problem. One simple way is to buy for your computer a set of the other kind of software. But this is a lot of money to spend just to deal with attachments.

Another way forward is to attempt conversions. There are ways of converting a document from one kind of software to another kind. So, for example, you might be able to convert a document written on a Mac word processor into Microsoft software. But these conversions are rather hit-or-miss: the result might be acceptable, but it might not be. Conversions are not a panacea.

Yet another procedure is to convert documents into something resembling plaintext. There is a format called **RichText**, which resembles plaintext but which usually retains italics, boldface, underlining, paragraphing and margins, at least. There is a good chance that your word processor will offer you the choice of a RichText version. RichText conversions will lose any graphics or pretty fonts or other fancy stuff, but at least the words will probably be readable by everybody – though I don't guarantee this, since my RichText conversions have occasionally turned out looking like a disaster in a spaghetti factory.

Again, if you need to send attachments, and you run into compatibility problems, it is best to talk directly to your recipients about what can usefully be done, and to try a few possibilities to see if you can settle on something that works.

6.4 SIZE

There are practical constraints on the size of an attachment. Size is measured in kilobytes (KB), and many mailers will refuse to carry attachments which exceed some maximum size. Most commentators advise you to keep an attachment below 50 KB. This is not large: an ordinary colour photograph may take up more space than this (colour photos are notorious for consuming huge amounts of space).

If you need to send an attachment which is much bigger than this, it is courteous and wise to get in touch with your recipients first and to check that what you propose is acceptable to them.

One way of handling a large attachment is to reduce its size by applying to it one of the several programs which compress a document (squeeze it into a much smaller space). Compressing your attachments saves space, but it adds another complication: your recipients must have the software required to restore the document to its original size. If they can't decompress it, they won't be able to read it, since a compressed document is unreadable.

On the whole, though, email attachments are not an appropriate way of sending large documents. Other and more suitable procedures exist, notably file-transfer programs. If you genuinely need to send large documents, then you should learn about file transfer.

Here is a true story. Not long ago, a friend of mine

went away for a week. On his return, he was surprised to find that his inbox contained only four emails, instead of the two hundred or so he had been expecting. But it didn't take long to find the explanation. Just after his departure, somebody had sent him an email attached to which was an *entire* Ph.D. thesis in uncompressed format. This gigantic attachment had taken up all the storage space available on his mailer, so that it could not accept any more mail, and all the mail arriving during the rest of the week had been rejected by his computer. Naturally, the sender had not bothered to check first with my friend as to whether he was willing to receive the thesis.

I hope it is obvious that the sender's behaviour was monumentally stupid and irresponsible. Make sure you are never guilty of such bad behaviour.

My friend was lucky that the attachment didn't freeze his mailer. If you send somebody an attachment which is too big for his mailer to store, his mailer may freeze and refuse to work at all. This is not the way to make friends.

In some cases, rather than trying to send a large attachment, you might be well advised to post the long document on the Web, and then simply to mail the URL (address) of the document. If you can do this, it makes life easy for everybody concerned. There are no compatibility problems with web pages – again, as long as you haven't made use of any flashy software.

A very small document can often be incorporated into the body of your email, so that you need not send an attachment at all. But, of course, if you are converting a document from some other format into the plaintext required for email, you must check the conversion and edit it as much as required to make it easy to read.

6.5 VIRUSES

The destructive programs called **viruses** are distributed from machine to machine by means of attachments to emails. Consequently, experienced users of computers are very wary of attachments. Many people and organizations simply refuse to open any attachments from strangers, because of the risk of viruses. So, if you need to send an attachment to someone you don't know, it's a good idea to introduce yourself first, to explain who you are and what you're up to. Once your recipients know you, *then* you can consider sending them an attachment. As usual, though, you should first explain the purpose of your attachment and get permission to send it.

For the same reason, it can be dangerous to forward (pass on) attachments you have received from strangers. You should never forward an attachment unless you are certain that it comes from a safe source.

6.6 EMPTY MESSAGES

There is one blunder which is so horrendously stupid and offensive, and yet so frequent, that I have decided to give it a section to itself. This is the empty message.

Almost once a week I open an email from a stranger and find myself staring at a blank window. What the malefactor has done is to send me an empty message with an attachment. Apparently he expects me to go to all the trouble of opening the attachment – which may not be a simple task – and wading through it, merely in order to find out what the mail is about and whether I'm even interested in reading it.

Well, if you've read the book this far, you can easily guess how I respond. When I see that empty window, I instantly reach for the Delete button. In half a second, that empty message is gone, and its unopened attachment is gone with it. There is no way on earth I am going to put up with such scandalously offensive behaviour.

You must never send anyone an empty message. No matter how wonderful your attachment is, you *must* provide a message explaining what the attachment is about and why you are sending it. And, of course, you must sign your message as usual: the idiots who send empty messages invariably fail to sign them, as well.

Attachments to empty messages are even more likely to carry viruses than other attachments, which is another reason for recipients not to open them. In fact, an attachment to an empty message is scarcely likely to be opened by anyone at all, apart perhaps from a few thoughtless beginners.

If you have ever been guilty of sending an empty message, I hope your ears are now burning with shame. In any case, don't do it again. The empty message is one of the most offensive misuses of email that I can conceive of.

6.7 AUDIO ATTACHMENTS

This is a rare problem, but I have known it to happen, so I guess there must be a few people out there who need to have this point explained to them. The point is simple: *Do not attach sound effects to your email.*

On an extremely rare occasion, it may be necessary or helpful to attach a sound recording to a professional posting in a specialist field. Otherwise, audio attachments are entirely out of order. Of all the things you can do to convince your recipients that you have a mental age of nine, attaching sound effects to your email is possibly top of the list.

6.8 COPYRIGHT

There is no legal problem when you attach a document you have created yourself. But you must not attach a document created by somebody else without the owner's permission. Doing so is a violation of copyright, and it's a quick way of getting yourself into trouble. (See chapter 10.)

Chapter summary:

- Before sending an attachment, check with your recipients
- Use only the most basic software to construct attachments
- Keep your attachments short
- Never send an empty message
- Never attach sound effects

7

Asking Questions

One of the most frequent uses of email is asking questions. Questions present some particular points of presentation and protocol.

7.1 CHECK BEFORE YOU ASK

Here is a piece of good advice: don't fire off a question by email until you have first tried to find the answer yourself.

Very commonly, I receive questions like this one:

What is the origin of the word 'calico'?

As it happens, *any* decent desk dictionary of English will explain the origins of English words. Reaching for the dictionary, finding the word and reading the account of its origin will chew up perhaps ninety seconds. You can't even boot up your computer that fast, and you may have to wait days for an answer to an email question.

Recently, a confused questioner emailed me wanting to know when and where paper and printing were invented. I don't know why he picked me, since such matters are far from my areas of competence. But the main point is that he had plainly made no effort to find the answers for himself before firing off his questions.

Information like this can be found in any encyclopedia. Having a computer on your desk does not cut you off from the world of printed books, and it is both foolish and rude to try to get a stranger to do the work which you could do for yourself in a couple of minutes.

Moreover, even if you don't have ready access to an encyclopedia, you can certainly consult the Web. Before you send off your question, spend a few minutes browsing the Web with your search engine.

The Web is anything but well organized, and there is no guarantee that the answer to any particular question can be found there. But the volume and variety of the information which is now available is truly astonishing.

Not long ago, I became curious about the origin of the name of that most quaintly named insect, the confused flour beetle. I reached for my search engine, and within a few seconds I found myself reading a detailed account of how the bug acquired its amusing name.

And recently I decided to investigate the humble kitchen blender. When I was a child, I was told by somebody that the blender had been invented by an American bandleader named Fred Waring. My attempts at looking this topic up in reference books were failures, so I turned to the Web. Again, it was only moments before I was reading the whole story of Fred Waring and his revolutionary machine.

The World Wide Web is a truly wonderful resource, and you should certainly learn how to use it. Unfortunately, the skilful and efficient use of search engines is a topic beyond the scope of this book, and I won't pursue the matter here.

But you will save yourself and other people a great deal of time if you simply get into the habit of looking at obvious sources before mailing questions. Consult the obvious reference books, and search the Web. Only if you find no joy in these searches should you then feel free to ask an electronic question.

There is more. If you are sending your question to an electronic service which deals in answering questions, there are two resources which you must check before sending in a question: FAQs and archives.

Many electronic resources maintain lists of **FAQs**, or Frequently Asked Questions. So, before using a service, look to see if it has a set of FAQs; if it has, then look at those FAQs to see if your question is among them. You may be asking your question for the first time, but you may be the eighty-seventh person to ask that question, and nobody will thank you for sending in a question to which the answer is already posted in the list of FAQs.

Here are some examples of questions which the panellists on Ask-a-Linguist get asked over and over and over again:

1. Is it wise to bring up my child bilingually?
2. Which is the oldest language?

3. What's the difference between a language and a dialect?
4. Which is the hardest language to learn?

(Just to make sure that you don't turn up on our list with one of these questions, here are the answers. (1) Yes; absolutely. (2) The question is meaningless: all languages are equally 'old'. (3) A dialect is a variety of a language which also has other varieties; a language is not a variety of anything larger than itself. (4) The language which is most different from your own.)

The other thing you should check for is **archives**. Some electronic resources maintain archives, which are files containing all the messages that have been received there. If archives exist, they will normally be accompanied by some device for searching them quickly and efficiently for particular topics. Again, it is good behaviour to search the archives before sending in a question, since the answer to your question might already be sitting there.

All of these things are good practice, and they are habits which you must cultivate if you want to be a responsible adult. Check the reference books; check the Web; check the FAQs; check the archives. *Then* you can send your question – not before. Firing off a question without doing these things is irresponsible and childish.

7.2 DECIDING WHO TO ASK

Once you have decided that you would like to ask a question by email, who should you ask? If you are lucky enough to find an electronic answering service in the right area, such as Ask-a-Linguist for languages and linguistics, then this issue is not a problem. But you may not be so lucky. What then?

A common approach here is to trawl the Web, looking for web pages devoted to the general area of the intended question. Suppose you are dying to ask a question about gender roles in small children. So, you put your search engine to work, and, after a while, you stumble across a web page which has some interesting things to say about this very subject. The page is owned by a certain Dr Alice Bloom in Canada. It seems clear that Dr Bloom knows a great deal about this subject, and therefore that she is a good bet to be able to answer your question. Should you therefore send her your question?

Well, look again at her web page. Does Dr Bloom invite readers to mail her with questions in her field? If so, there should be no problem in sending her your question. If this is not the case, does she at least provide a link to her email on her web page? If she does, then she is tacitly inviting you to mail her, so you can go ahead with confidence.

But suppose you find no such encouragement. Well, you can't mail her at all without her address, but perhaps a little more trawling of the Web will turn up her email address on another site – maybe her university's home page. Now what?

Now it gets tricky. Dr Bloom is clearly somebody who will probably be able to answer your question, but she has so far given you no particular reason to believe that she welcomes questions from strangers out of the blue. Should you go ahead anyway?

There is no easy answer to this. But, if you want to ask your question, you don't have much choice, so you may as well go ahead and ask. But listen.

Approaching a total stranger for help out of the blue is an imposition. You are asking someone you have never met to devote time and effort to helping you. And it is a safe bet that Dr Bloom is a busy woman with little time to spare for strangers: she does not spend her afternoons yawning at her desk, hoping that someone will brighten up her empty day with an email.

Now, most people are courteous, and most people will try to help, especially with questions within their specialist fields, about which they are undoubtedly enthusiastic. In principle, therefore, Dr Bloom will probably be happy to tell you a little something about her favourite subject.

But you must take the greatest care in approaching a stranger for help. You must demonstrate that you *deserve* help. First, you should briefly apologize for approaching her at all. Second, you should briefly explain who you are and why you are asking your question. Third, you must make every effort to write a question which is as clear as you can make it, and you must put your question into the very best standard English you can muster. Of course, you should take such care with *every* serious email you send, but you should be especially careful when you approach a stranger. Here is a suggested version of the question:

[subject line] Q: Gender roles complete by age two?

Dear Dr Bloom,

Forgive me for approaching you out of the blue, but you are my best hope for answering a question that is bothering me. I will shortly be starting a university degree in social psychology, and I have a particular interest in gender issues.

An article in a popular magazine assures me that children in western countries have been steered into their adult gender roles, completely and irreversibly, by the age of two. Is this true? Can you suggest some serious and reliable reading on this subject?

Thank you in advance,

Christina Maddox

chris.maddox@plover.net

This is a good effort, and it stands an excellent chance of eliciting a friendly and helpful reply from Dr Bloom.

Just for comparison, here is a very bad attempt at asking the same question:

[subject line] children

Do children acquire their gender roles by age two?

This version gets everything wrong. The subject line is useless; the question here is abrupt and rude; there is no signature; and the questioner is seemingly taking it for granted that she has a right to demand an answer from Dr Bloom. Dr Bloom is unlikely to see it that way. Even though she enjoys talking about her subject, she may well decide that this anonymous question is too impolite to merit a reply. And who would blame her?

7.3 SUBJECT LINES

When you are asking a question, there is a convention of marking this fact in the subject line by typing 'Q:' at the beginning. Here is a sample subject line for a question on raising children bilingually:

Q: Raising children bilingually

This lets your recipients know at once that you are asking a question about the topic you have identified. As always, writing subject lines that are as clear and explicit as possible makes life easier for the people you are mailing.

However, this convention can be ignored in one context. When you are sending a question to an electronic service which accepts *only* questions, then it is obvious that you are asking a question, and that 'Q:' can be omitted. So, for example, if you are sending your question to Ask-a-Linguist, an electronic service which offers to answer questions on language and linguistics, you can just write the following subject line:

Raising children bilingually

If in doubt, use the 'Q:'. Nobody ever got shot for being overly careful and thoughtful.

Now, we talked about writing good subject lines in chapter 3, but the topic is worth returning to here. When you ask a question, choose a subject line that identifies the nature of your question as explicitly as possible. On Ask-a-Linguist, every one of the several dozen queries we see each week is a question about some aspect of language, and a subject line like Question or Language is completely useless – yet quite a few questions arrive with precisely these futile headings. Nor is it any better to fill the subject line with something lame like Just wondering or Can you help me?

Suppose you are asking a question about the Spanish subjunctive. Then, of course, your subject line should probably read Spanish subjunctive. To me, this seems blindingly obvious, but it is amazing how many people try to get by with something unhelpful like Spanish, or with something even worse. Likewise, if you are asking a question – not on Ask-a-Linguist, I hope – about recent suggestions of a tenth planet in our solar system, then something like A tenth planet? will probably serve your purposes admirably, while a feeble effort like Planets or New discoveries is of no use to any reader.

No member of the Ask-a-Linguist panel can hope to answer every question that arrives, and I appreciate it when the subject line tells me at once whether this is a question I can probably answer or not. If I see a subject like Technical terms in Urdu or The language of Eliot's poetry, then I know at once that I can't say anything helpful, so I can leave that question to my colleagues, and pass on to the questions I can answer.

If you use email to ask questions – or even if you don't – learn to provide subject lines which are as clear and explicit as they can possibly be. Feeble or useless subject lines only make life a little more difficult for the people you are mailing.

Here is a little practice. Suppose you are sending each of the three questions below. What subject line would you attach to each?

1. I once read that the game of baseball is mentioned by Jane Austen in one of her novels. Is this true? If so, where can I find the reference?

2. Everybody knows that America is named after Amerigo Vespucci. But I've read conflicting accounts of Vespucci's achievements. Some accounts dismiss him as a charlatan who embroidered his insignificant voyages, while others credit him with important discoveries. Is there a definitive view?

3. A popular book I'm reading claims that the Amazon once flowed westward into the Pacific, but that the rise of the Andes blocked the river and forced it to flow the other way, into the Atlantic. Is this true? If so, where can I find a serious scientific account of the matter?

Ponder these questions a moment, and then decide what subject lines you would provide. I trust that you are wise enough by now to refrain from feeble efforts like Baseball and Vespucci and Amazon, not to mention pathetic efforts like America or Question or Can you help? Have you made up your mind? All right; here are my suggestions: (1) Q: Baseball in Jane Austen; (2) Q: Amerigo Vespucci's real achievements; (3) Q: Has the Amazon been turned round?

How did you do? Are your suggestions explicit and to the point? Can a stranger reading your subject line tell at once what you are asking about?

(In case your curiosity is getting the better of you, here are the answers. (1) Yes; the game of 'base ball' is mentioned by Jane Austen in *Northanger Abbey*. This is thought to be the first published mention of the game. (2) The jury is still out on Vespucci. For a long time, he was generally regarded as a liar, but historians seem to be gradually coming round to the view that many of his stories were true. (3) Yes; the Amazon flowed into the Pacific until the rise of the Andes, about 15 million years ago, blocked its flow. The river turned into a gigantic freshwater lake until it finally broke through to the Atlantic, about 10 million years ago. You can find accounts of these events on a number of websites.

By the way, finding those sites on the Amazon will provide an excellent test of your skill in using a search engine. Any attempt to type in 'amazon' plus anything else at all will typically return a huge number of hits on the giant Internet bookseller Amazon.com, and you will need to be resourceful to find a way of removing these unwanted hits, so that you can get to the sites you are looking for.)

7.4 WRITING GOOD QUESTIONS

Quite a few of the questions that reach my inbox are so poorly written that I honestly cannot understand what the questioner is trying to find out. Here is a genuine example, slightly adapted:

> In gender communictaion there is a pattern of domi-
> nance. Are there any studies that show these patterns?

Well, to start with, you can see that this questioner has not even bothered to read her own question. If she had read it, she would have spotted and corrected the obvious typo, and she might also have done something about the clash between the singular form *a pattern* in the first sentence and the suddenly plural form *these patterns* in the second. But there are far more serious problems.

What on earth is *gender communication*? These words are completely meaningless. No doubt the questioner has something in mind, but she hasn't made the slightest effort to explain what that is, and so I am helpless. I might hazard the wild guess that she means 'conversations between men and women', but my guess might be miles from what she is trying to talk about. Anyway, it doesn't matter whether my guess is right or wrong, because now the questioner has another obstacle for me.

What does she mean by *a pattern of dominance*? This wording is so vague that it might mean almost anything. Who or what is supposed to be dominating who or what? The questioner gives me no clue, and again I am helpless.

Finally, there is yet another obscurity. In her first sentence, the questioner asserts flatly that this dominance, whatever it is, exists. Apparently the reality of this dominance is an established fact, one whose reality is beyond discussion. But then, in her second sentence, she seems to be asking whether there exists any evidence for the reality of such dominance! So, she first asserts that this dominance exists, and then asks if there is any evidence that it exists. What on earth is she playing at? And what in the name of sanity is she trying to find out?

Questions like this one are all too common. They turn up because so many questioners simply cannot be bothered to spend a little time in thinking carefully about what they are trying to find out and in composing clear and explicit questions.

The questioner who sent in the question above had clearly just dashed it off and sent it in, without editing it and without even thinking about it. The result is an incomprehensible question which will receive no useful answers, and in fact no answers at all beyond perhaps 'What are you talking about?'

Now, I still don't know what this questioner is asking about. But I'll make a guess, and compose a question that asks more successfully about my guess:

I have read that, in conversations between men and women, the male speakers regularly dominate the conversations in some conspicuous manner. Are there any

studies which confirm this assertion, and which identify the nature of this male dominance?

Now, at least this is a clear and explicit question. No
reader will have any trouble understanding what is
being asked here, and any reader who knows about the
subject will be able to provide an informative reply.
But *is* this what the original questioner was asking
about? I still don't know.

Here is another genuine example, again slightly
adapted:

Would like the word 'Roys' translated into Welsh Gaelic

There is more sloppiness here: the questioner has not
even bothered to write a complete sentence. But again
there are more serious problems.

What in heaven's name is the word *Roys*? The only
Roy in English is the male given name, as in Roy Rogers
– but such names don't normally have plural forms.
Moreover, names don't usually have translations: the
name *Bill Clinton* is still *Bill Clinton* in Italian or Polish.

So, again I am entirely at a loss to know what the
questioner is trying to find out. His question makes
no sense at all, and this time I can't even come up with
a wild guess.

Just to put the icing on the cake, there is no such
language as *Welsh Gaelic*. Perhaps the questioner has
Welsh in mind, or perhaps Gaelic, or perhaps something else altogether. Perhaps he himself has no idea
what he is talking about. Who knows? How can anyone
tell?

Once again, the questioner's failure to devote a few minutes to the business of constructing a careful and explicit question has resulted in an incomprehensible mess that will receive no answer. And what is the point of firing off a question which nobody can understand? Do you begin to see why haste in composing emails is a bad idea, and why careful planning and writing is essential?

Can you face one more of these? Here's another genuine example, just as it arrived in my inbox:

> I recently noticed the Pyramid floor in Memphis labled with the words 'The Pyramid'. This seems to be an inapproprate use of the article 'the' since it is apparently labling the object. Is this proper or should it more appropriately be labled just Pyramid or Pyramid Arena?

I must have read this a dozen times now, and I still have not the faintest idea what this questioner is asking. And this time the text is so far from intelligible that I can't even pick out the problems with any confidence. But I'll try.

What do you suppose *the Pyramid floor in Memphis* might be? Are we talking about Memphis, Tennessee, or about Memphis, Egypt? The questioner fails to say. The word *pyramid* suggests Egypt, but *Pyramid Arena* sounds more like a night spot in Tennessee – and there are no pyramids in Memphis, Egypt. The questioner seems to be taking it for granted that everybody in the world is intimately acquainted with the pleasure spots of Memphis, Tennessee, or with the archaeological sites of Memphis, Egypt – but I've never set foot in either place. What do you suppose the phrase *the object* is meant to denote? I certainly can't guess. And it certainly doesn't help that the questioner tosses the hapless little pronoun *it* around in promiscuous fashion, applying it first to the word *the* (I think, anyway) and then to the mysterious building (well, I *think* it's a building, though the questioner has not bothered to say so).

Bear in mind that the people who sent in these messages were not simply idlers trying to waste everybody's time. They had genuine questions in their minds, and they genuinely wanted their questions answered. And they genuinely thought that they had asked questions which the people at the other end would easily be able to answer. But their abject failure to expend the necessary time and effort in framing their questions with sufficient care has led to disaster in all cases. And I can assure you that I receive equally incomprehensible questions almost every week.

People working in other circumstances report other kinds of useless requests. The email commentator Kaitlin Duck Sherwood, who used to work in a university, reports that she was forever receiving requests like this one:

Please send me information about your university.

As she remarks acidly, this kind of mail gives her no clue at all about what is wanted. List of degrees offered? Application deadlines? Number of students? Number of buildings? History? Is she being asked for paper documents or for the university's URL? Who knows?

If you can't write a better email than this one, there is hardly any point in trying to write an email at all. You are simply wasting everybody's time.

7.5 PROVIDING A CONTEXT

A common failing in asking electronic questions is the absence of a context. When you are framing your question, you know exactly the context in which your question has arisen. But the people at the other end don't know anything about that context if you don't tell them, and this can make life very difficult for them.

Here is a bad example which is quite typical of many of the questions I receive:

What is the meaning of the term 'specified reference'?

Well, I don't know. This is not a standard term in my field, and I can't find it in any of the specialist dictionaries on my shelf.

What has happened? Well, I can surmise as follows. The questioner is reading a particular book by a particular writer, and that book uses the term I am being asked about. The questioner has foolishly jumped to the conclusion that this is a term which is universally known and used in linguistics, and so he has failed to provide any context. Bad move, since my colleagues and I now have practically no chance of coming up with a useful answer.

Here is an illustration of what the questioner *should* have written:

I am reading P. W. Frobisher's book _Words Into Words_, which deals with the theory and practice of translation. In several places, the author uses the term 'specified reference' without explaining it. Here is a typical example, from page 97: 'Here the rendering of French "la paix" with the bare English "peace" would lose the specified reference of the original.' Can you explain the meaning of this term?

This effort is very much better. There is still no guarantee that we can provide a good answer, but at least now we understand the question, and so we have a *chance* of saying something helpful.

This shortcoming is really very frequent in questions about terms. Unless you are *certain* that the term you are asking about is universally used among the people you are mailing, you should be careful to provide as much context as you can.

But the same problem can arise in other kinds of questions. Here is a genuine question which I received a few days ago:

Do women speak faster than men?

Does this question look straightforward? Well, it's not. Which women? In which society? In which social group? In what contexts? The questioner appears to be taking it for granted that the answer must be a plain 'yes' or 'no' for all the women in the world, in all languages, on all occasions. But the world is not so simple. Unless the questioner wants to receive an essay on sex differences in speech all across the world – which nobody is going to provide anyway – she should narrow down her question to the cases she is interested in:

> Is there any evidence that women in the English-speaking countries typically speak faster than men? Does the answer appear to vary with social class or context or with other variables?

This version is more focused and more professional, and it is more likely to attract some informative replies.

The next time someone tells you that careful composition and editing are out of place with emails, you can smile quietly to yourself and dismiss your would-be adviser as a fool.

7.6 MULTIPLE QUESTIONS

As a general rule, you should ask only *one* question in a single message. It is permissible to ask two, or at most three, closely related questions at one time, but no more. So, something like this is acceptable:

> What is the origin of the name 'Eskimo'? Why is this name now widely regarded as offensive? And what are the differences among the words 'Inuit', 'Inuktitut' and 'Yupik'?

These are closely related questions on a single topic, and grouping them like this will perturb nobody. But this is enough for one email.

You must avoid the kind of excess illustrated by my next example, which is very similar to several real questions I have received; the mysterious terms are technical terms in my field of linguistics:

> Can you tell me the meanings of the words 'phone', 'phoneme', 'allophone', 'morph', 'morpheme', 'allomorph', 'alternant', 'cranberry morpheme', 'portmanteau morph', 'zero morph', 'phrase', 'clause', 'main clause', 'subordinate clause', 'complement clause' and 'matrix clause'?

This deluded questioner does not appear to understand the difference between a human being and a dictionary. In any case, he is being wholly unreasonable. Asking for the definition of one term is fine, but asking about every term you've run into this week is intolerable. A question of this kind will receive no reply except this one: 'Go and look in a dictionary.'

It gets worse. Some time ago, I had occasion to answer a question from a high-school student. Seemingly delighted with my answer, he then came back to me with a list of almost forty questions, which he had obviously just dreamed up while staring at his computer screen. Apparently he was under the impression that I have nothing better to do all day than to sit in front of my computer and laboriously answer long strings of dumb questions from dozy high-school students. Naturally, I didn't even bother to reply.

7.7 DEMANDING A QUICK REPLY

One of the most offensive things you can do, when asking a question – or in any email at all – is to demand a rapid reply. It always amazes me how many emails arrive in my inbox with a final sentence like Please reply to me quickly or I need an answer right away.

Remember – the people you are mailing are *busy*. They are courteous, and they will reply to you as soon as they reasonably can. Demanding a quick response will *not* get you an answer any sooner, and in fact it may have the opposite effect. Some readers may bridle at your rudeness in demanding a fast answer, and decide that your behaviour does not deserve a reply at all.

Don't ask for a rapid response. If you need the information right away, that's *your* problem. Anyway, have you already checked the obvious reference books? And have you searched the Web? No? Why not?

7.8 HOMEWORK

Students in schools and universities are often tempted to use email questions to get answers to their homework. This is potentially dangerous.

Your teacher or your course tutor will probably be pleased if you search the Web in order to find the information that you need to complete an assignment. But asking other people to do your work for you is a very different matter.

If you are thinking of doing this, you must first obtain your teacher's permission. This permission may not be granted, since your teacher may consider it improper for you simply to ask someone else to do your work for you.

If you do get permission, then you must make it clear in your question that you are seeking help with an assignment. Don't be coy: spell it out. Explain that you are asking for help with your homework, and explain that your teacher has given you permission to do this.

Finally, if you get any useful answers, make sure that you acknowledge the assistance you have received, expressly and fully, when you hand in your work.

You *must* do these things. Failure to do them is dishonest. To be blunt, you are cheating if you are not completely open and honest with all concerned about what you are doing.

There is another point to be considered. You know by now that I am on the panel of Ask-a-Linguist. Several years ago, I was startled to see a question arrive which was exactly one of the questions which I had just set my first-year students for homework – and the name at the end of the question was that of one of my students.

Well, of course I gave him a flea in his ear. And then I pointed out to him that, if he had done the assigned reading in the textbook, he would have found the answer he was looking for.

Asking someone else to do your work for you is cheating, even when you ask electronically. Don't do it.

There is one circumstance in which it is legitimate to approach strangers for help with your homework. Assuming your teacher has given you permission to do this, it is fine to approach strangers and to ask them to recommend work which you can consult. So, it is acceptable to approach me with an email like this one:

I'm writing an essay on the differences between human language and animal communication. Can you recommend any useful reading on this subject?

But it is completely out of order, when you are writing this essay, to mail me in this fashion:

> What are the principal differences between human language and animal communication?

Now you are asking me to do your work for you. And that is wrong.

I can't resist quoting one more question which arrived recently at Ask-a-Linguist:

> I am in my third year of a linguistics degree and must come up with a title for a 6000 word essay. I was wondering if anyone had any interesting ideas for a possible topic?

I think it is safe to say that requests of this kind are frowned upon. It might have been acceptable if the questioner had named a specific area, such as first-language acquisition or the grammar of Spanish, and asked for suggestions within that limited domain. But asking for titles on *any subject at all* is absurd.

7.9 IDENTIFYING YOUR COUNTRY

Many of the questions I get asked by email can only be sensibly answered if I know what country the questioner lives in. Consider questions like these, both of which are similar to many of the questions I see:

> At which universities can I study Sanskrit?

Where can I find an importer which imports Spanish liqueurs?

Now, is the first questioner really interested in hearing about degrees in Sanskrit offered by universities in Australia or Sweden? It is certainly possible to study Sanskrit in India, but is a questioner who lives in Liverpool or Chicago likely to be eager to travel to India to do a university degree?

Likewise, if the second questioner lives in Sydney or Las Vegas, is she probably dying to find out about importers in South Africa or in Japan?

You see the point. Questions like these are impossible to answer if the questioners fail to identify their countries – but in fact *most questioners* fail to do this. I'm not sure whether they are just thoughtless, or whether they dozily believe that theirs is the only country in the world which is connected to the Internet.

So, when you ask a question, look at it carefully and decide whether you need to identify your country. Don't assume that the name of your country is obvious. Some email addresses carry two-letter country codes, like .uk for Britain and .ca for Canada, but most addresses lack these codes, and carry instead only something wholly uninformative like .com or .net. Anyway, not all users will realize that .de is Germany, or that .my is Malaysia.

7.10 THANK-YOU MESSAGES

If you ask a question, and somebody mails you an answer, it is common courtesy to thank the respondent. Nothing fancy is called for: just a plain 'Thank you' will do. As always, email is not disconnected from the rest of the world, and what is courteous and proper in dealing with people in other contexts remains courteous and proper in electronic contexts.

Oh, and leave it at that. It *might* be acceptable to return to your respondent with one follow-up question, but no more. Don't do what some people do, and try to treat the respondent as your permanent source of information.

Chapter summary:

- Check other resources before asking a question
- Provide an *informative* subject line, preceded by 'Q:'
- Frame your question carefully and thoughtfully
- Provide a good context for your question
- Avoid multiple questions
- Don't demand a quick reply
- Don't ask somebody to do your homework for you
- Identify your country when this matters
- Thank your respondents

8
Replying and Forwarding

8.1 HEADERS

When you receive an email, you should find that the body of the text is preceded by a series of lines of information. These lines are called the **header**. The header tells you who sent the message, who it was sent to, and when it was sent. As a rule, it also carries the full subject line provided by the sender, no matter how long that subject line is. So, a typical header looks like this:

Sent: 18 August 2004, 15.34
From: Andrew Holt <a.holt@shockley.co.uk>
To: Cynthia Drummond <Cynthia.Drummond@jdg.
co.uk>
Subject: Alterations to our winter catalogue

You can see the value of the header. It provides a great deal of valuable information in a small space. Among other things, the sender's name and email address are spelled out here. This information may not be easy to recover from any other source. Moreover, if you print a copy of the mail, the header will be printed as well. This is important, because the subject line and any other lines which stand above the body of the message often fail to print.

There is one common variation here. Many mailers, instead of repeating the header of the original message, will delete that header and replace it with a line like this one:

On 18 August 2004 Andrew Holt <a.holt@shockley. co.uk> wrote:

This arrangement is substantially less informative than the first one, but it is very common. If your mailer offers you a choice, you are advised to prefer the first style.

Unfortunately, some mailers have the very bad habit of stripping (deleting) the header altogether. This is bad, because such stripping removes information which you may not be able to find anywhere else. Recall from chapter 2 that I advised you strongly to put your full name and your email address at the end of every email. Doing so ensures that this vital information will be present in your email, even if your recipient's mailer strips the header.

8.2 DECIDING WHETHER TO REPLY

Suppose you receive an email that seems to call for a reply. The need for a reply may be obvious if the other person has carefully inserted the notation 'Q:' (for 'question') or 'Req:' (for 'request') into the subject line of the mail you are looking at, but, even without such overt markings, you may decide that a response is appropriate.

Before you begin typing a reply, you should first check the rest of your mail. There is always the possibility that the other person has sent you a second message saying 'Forget it!', in which case you will be wasting your time in composing a reply. Second, the sender may have discovered a blunder in the original message and therefore sent a corrected version, which is the one you are now meant to reply to. Third, if the original message was sent to several people, and not just to you personally, it may be that someone else has already sent the same reply that you were about to send. Checking your mail before replying can save you a couple of pointless messages a week.

If the message appears to be outstandingly important, but you don't have the time to reply to it right away, you might consider sending a brief response just to confirm that you have received it and to assure the sender that you will deal with it as quickly as you can.

One last point. This is probably not something that you will often need to worry about. However, every once in a while, you may find a forged message or a spoof message in your inbox. Such a message will carry the name of someone who is more or less familiar to you, or else the name of someone who appears to be in a position of authority. The object will be to make a fool of you by eliciting an innocent response to the phony message.

In most cases, you can spot the fake merely by

exercising a little judgement and common sense. If the message appears to be completely out of character for the person whose name it carries, or if it appears to be outstandingly unreasonable in content, then you are probably looking at a forged message, and you should simply ignore it, or, if it appears disturbing, report it to your system administrator.

8.3 THE MECHANICS OF REPLYING

In most cases, you will reply to a message by clicking on the Reply button on your mailer. When you do this, several things will normally happen. First, a new window will pop up on your screen, ready for you to type your reply into. (But see below for a possible variation here.) Second, one or more email addresses will be automatically inserted into the address line. Third, if there were any ccs in the original message, these will be repeated on your cc line. Fourth, the subject line of the original message will be copied into your subject line, but preceded by the word 'Re:', which means 'concerning'. Fifth, the text of the original message, including its header, will appear in the window, with each line preceded by a special character, usually the right angle bracket, >. Finally, your ordinary signature – assuming you have constructed one – will appear as well. Let's talk about these things.

The window needs no discussion, but the address line does. The first thing you should do is to check the address line to see who your reply is going to go to (so far). If the original message was sent to several people, then quite possibly the addresses of all these people will appear. Do you really want to send your reply to all of them? If so, fine; but, if not, you must carefully delete the addresses you don't want. Doing this is important: it is highly inconsiderate to fill people's inboxes with messages that are of no interest to them.

At my university, it occasionally happens that a routine question from the administration building is sent to fifty or two hundred of the academic staff. I will amuse no one if I send my reply to all fifty or two hundred of my colleagues when no one but the questioner has any interest in my answer.

The same goes with the cc line. Any addresses listed here should likewise be deleted unless you decide that you really do need to send your reply to these people.

However, some mailers work slightly differently. On these mailers, when you click on the Reply button, you don't immediately get a reply window. Instead, you get a little window containing a list of all the addresses to which your reply will be addressed or cced. If you're not satisfied with this list, you can edit it by clicking on the addresses with your mouse. Once you are happy, you click on 'OK' or 'Done', and *then* you will get the reply window, just as I have described it.

Most mailers have a Reply All button as well as a Reply button. If you click on Reply All, you will probably discover that your reply is being sent to every address the mailer can find in the original message. Use this option with care.

Now to the subject line. Whatever the original subject line was, it should be copied automatically onto the subject line of your reply, but preceded by the word Re:, which is universally understood as marking a reply to an earlier message. So, if the subject line of the original message was Next Tuesday's meeting, then the subject line of your reply will read Re: Next Tuesday's meeting.

If this 'Re:' fails to appear, then something may be wrong with the settings of your mailer program, and you should check the settings for outgoing mail, which you will probably find under **preferences**. Meanwhile, I'm afraid you must add the 'Re:' by hand, since its presence is essential.

It is this ever-present 'Re:' that identifies genuine replies in the inboxes of your recipients. And this is why any email with the subject line Reply to your query can be identified instantly as a piece of dishonest junk mail and deleted without the trouble of opening it. No genuine reply ever has such a subject line.

If the message you are replying to already contains this element 'Re:', then your reply should *not* add a second instance of it. So, if you are replying to a message with the subject line Re: Next Tuesday's meeting, then the subject line of your reply should still be displayed as Re: Next Tuesday's meeting. This should happen automatically. If instead your mailer should come up with Re: Re: Next Tuesday's meeting, then you should carefully delete one instance of that 'Re:'. Otherwise, after a few messages back and forth, you will all be looking at a subject line which runs Re: Re: Re: Re: Re:, and so on. This is a rare problem, but I have known it to happen.

In the window created for your reply, you will see

the entire text of the message you are replying to, including its header. Every line of this text should be preceded by a special marker. In practice, the marker which is used almost universally is the right angle bracket, >. So, suppose the original message was this:

Sent: 14 March 2004
From: Angela Thorne <Angela.Thorne@albatross.co.uk>
To: Richard Briscoe <rwbriscoe@chem.neasden.ac.uk>
Subject: Chinese rights to your textbook

Richard,

We have received a request from a publisher in the People's Republic of China to publish a Chinese translation of your textbook in China. The royalties will be modest, but think of the fame! Are you happy to agree to this? If so, I'll post you details of the agreement.

Best, Angela

Angela Thorne
Commissioning Editor
Albatross Publishers
602 Old Market Street
London EC4 9JY

This will appear in your reply window as follows:

> Sent: 14 March 2004
> From: Angela Thorne <Angela.Thorne@albatross.co.uk>

> To: Richard Briscoe <rwbriscoe@chem.neasden.ac.uk>
> Subject: Chinese rights to your textbook
>
> Richard,
>
> We have received a request from a publisher in the
> People's Republic of China to publish a Chinese
> translation of your textbook in China. The royalties
> will be modest, but think of the fame! Are you happy to
> agree to this? If so, I'll post you details of the
> agreement.
>
> Best, Angela
>
> Angela Thorne
> Commissioning Editor
> Albatross Publishers
> 602 Old Market Street
> London EC4 9JY

Again, if the angle brackets fail to appear, then you
should check the settings for outgoing mail on your
mailer. Those brackets are important. As we will see
later, they are of crucial value in distinguishing the
words of the original message from the words of your
reply. Without the brackets, your readers may become
hopelessly confused as to what belongs to the original
message and what belongs to the reply.

I am told that a few mailers fail to provide those
crucial brackets. If your mailer fails to provide them,
this is an excellent reason for buying a new mailer.

If the message you are replying to already contains

a passage marked off by angle brackets, then your reply will add a second layer of brackets, and each line of that passage will be set off by two angle brackets, >>. This goes on for ever, with each new reply adding another layer of angle brackets. After a while, these brackets will make the lines too long to fit into a mailer window, and the result may be almost unreadable. Try to avoid this fate by not quoting things without limit.

Your signature will be attached to your reply, just as you have constructed it. But there is one possible problem here. If you are thinking of quoting part of the message in your reply, then you really want your signature to appear at the *end* of your reply, *after* the quoted text set off in angle brackets. This way, your reply will consist of the quoted part of the original, followed by your words of response, followed finally by your signature. But some mailers insist on putting your signature at the top of the reply window, *before* the quoted text. If your mailer does this, and you can't set the mailer to put your signature at the end, then you will have to use the cut-and-paste feature to move your signature to the end whenever you want to quote from the original text in your reply. If you often want to quote from the original message, this constant cutting-and-pasting is a flaming nuisance, and it might justify buying a new mailer.

8.4 EXPLAINING WHAT YOU'RE REPLYING TO

It is crucial to make it completely clear just what it is you're replying to. Nobody wants to open a mail from you and read something like Yes or I'm afraid I can't do it or Has Angela agreed to this?, staring out of an otherwise blank window. Even with a good subject line – which the original sender may have failed to provide – such a message may be wholly unintelligible. You can't safely assume that the sender knows instantly just which of possibly many emails you are replying to, or that he recalls every word of that email.

At the very least, then, you will need either to provide a few words of explanation as to what you are replying to or to quote a couple of lines from the original message. If the original message was very short – no more than about six lines – then you can quote it in full.

But don't quote the original message pointlessly. We come now to one of the central skills of emailing: *you must delete all unwanted material*. It is dreadful practice to include in your reply the entire text of the message you are replying to when that text serves no function. Nobody wants to open an email and stare at two hundred lines quoted from an earlier mail, with your three-line reply tacked on somewhere. Anybody who has to wade through this kind of mess is going to become very annoyed, and some people may just give up.

It is a ghastly experience to watch an exchange between two people who have never learned to delete the text they are replying to. After a couple of messages in each direction, the entire correspondence is strung out at length at the end of every new email. Such a collection is a ridiculous waste of storage space and money. Don't let this happen to you. Learn to delete.

You may think you are avoiding the problem by

putting your reply at the beginning, with the entire original message trailing after it. But this is bad practice for another reason. Placing your reply before the words you are replying to is called 'top-posting', and top-posting can be very annoying. Look at the bad example below.

There is something to be said for all three options, but on balance I am convinced that the second option will be the least costly.

> We will soon have to make a decision about providing
> technical support for our computing facilities. As you
> know, our budget is limited, and good technical staff
> don't grow on trees. The Working Party has been
> investigating the possibilities, and it has identified
> three priorities in terms of which our final decision
> should be . . . [goes on for some time]

This reply has been provided in a vacuum, and any recipient who has not memorized the original message will be baffled by it. That hapless recipient will now have to wade through the original message to find out what the first three lines mean.

Avoid top-posting. It will earn you no friends. The proper way of replying to a long message is explained in the next section.

8.5 QUOTING FROM THE ORIGINAL MESSAGE

Sometimes the message you are replying to consists of several points, one after another, and you may find it necessary to respond to each point in turn. In this case, it is best to quote one point at a time, and to add your response after that quotation, before moving on to the next point. As a result, your reply will consist of alternating passages, one quoted passage set off by angle brackets, and then one passage written by you in response.

If you find that you don't need to respond to some part of the original, then don't waste space by quoting that part: delete it, and insert the word [snip] to show that material has been deleted. If you find that you can usefully delete a short sequence from the middle of a passage, then delete it and insert [. . .] to show that a short piece of text has been deleted.

While you are doing all these things, be careful to ensure that every line quoted from the original message is marked by an angle bracket. Sometimes a few of the angle brackets get lost during editing, and you must insert additional angle brackets by hand, in order to keep the structure of your reply clear.

Let's look at an example of this. Suppose you have received the message below:

On 7 May 2004 Steve Baxter <s.v.baxter@cyclops. co.uk> wrote:

We've just heard from the head office about the new procedures for assessing employees. They've put forward several proposals, and they'd like to have your comments on them.

1. Each employee to be assessed every 12 months, instead
of every 18 months, as now.

2. Assessors to include immediate superior and two colleagues, instead of one colleague, as now.

3. Assessees to provide a written account of their own achievements since the last assessment.

Steve Baxter

Your reply might look like this:

> On 7 May 2004 Steve Baxter <s.v.baxter@cyclops.
co.uk>
> wrote:

[snip]

[comments on new assessment proposals]

> 1. Each employee to be assessed every 12 months
[. . .]

Good from the company's point of view, but it won't be popular. Assessment is unpleasant and time-consuming, and there will be resistance to making it more frequent.

> 2. Assessors to include immediate superior and two
> colleagues [. . .]

A good idea, and most people will like being assessed by two colleagues, but it will double the amount of work for everybody – another reason not to make assessment more frequent.

> 3. Assessees to provide a written account of their own
> achievements since the last assessment.

This idea will be very popular with high flyers. Weaker people will hate it. Is this what the company wants?

Madeleine Stephenson
Maddy.Stephenson@cyclops.co.uk

Observe how clearly the structure of the reply emerges from the screen (represented here by the page). If the writer had instead quoted the entire original message, followed by her entire response, then the result would be much harder to follow. And note also how useful those angle brackets are in setting off portions of the original message. Without the brackets, the structure of the response would be much less visible.

Another point to notice is that the writer has deleted as much of the original message as she could without losing the essential material. You should do the same. Quoting huge chunks of the original message to no point is thoughtless and inconsiderate. As always, an email should be as brief as it can be while getting its job done effectively, and a reply is no different in this respect from any other mail.

Some commentators propose a rule of thumb: in any reply, at least half the lines should be yours. This is a good notion to keep in mind, but, of course, it doesn't mean that a reply which is 50 per cent quoted material is always a good idea.

Finally, observe that the respondent has added these words: [comments on new assessment proposals]. Such brief words of introduction are excellent practice. Instead of tediously quoting a possibly long passage explaining the point of what follows, you can simply delete that long passage and replace it with a few brisk words of explanation. Your readers will thank you.

8.6 CLARITY AND EXPLICITNESS

A reply, like any piece of writing, should be framed carefully and thoughtfully. A hasty and offhand reply may mislead or even baffle the person you are replying to.

Suppose someone is replying to this message:

In line with our recent decision that every member of staff should create and maintain a personal web page, we have arranged for our support staff to offer a course in HTML, the markup language in which web pages are constructed. The course will be given twice a week, on Wednesday afternoons and on Friday afternoons, beginning in the week of 27 March and running for six weeks. No more than twelve people can be accommodated on each day. Please let us know whether you

need to enrol on the course and which day you prefer.
Please let us know also whether you use a Mac or a PC.

And suppose this is the reply:

Yes; I'd like to do it, and I use a Mac.

This hasty response has failed to answer one of the questions in the first message, and now there will have to be another time-consuming exchange of messages in order to extract the missing information. This has happened either because the respondent has not read the message carefully enough or because he has dashed off his reply with too little care.

Since you are no doubt reading this book carefully, you are probably surprised to be told that anyone could reply to a message in such an obviously inadequate manner. But in fact this sort of thing happens all the time. People are busy; they read their mail hastily; they make assumptions about the content of their mail; and they construct their responses with far less care and attention than is appropriate.

Of course, the original questioner could have constructed the first message more carefully, by enumerating the three questions being asked. Doing this would have greatly reduced the likelihood of careless and defective replies. But it is unrealistic to expect that every email you receive will be impeccably composed, and you need to learn to deal with real messages in the real world.

Consider another example:

We are contemplating the purchase of a new Photon photocopier to replace our existing machine, which is seven years old and which has been breaking down with distressing frequency. The Photon costs about £4,700, including VAT, a price which will virtually exhaust our equipment budget for the year. Buying the copier will mean that we can't buy a scanner this year. The Photon offers graded enlargement to 200% and reduction to 50%; double-sided copying from both single- and double-sided originals; copying on A4 or A3 paper; collating and optional stapling of multi-page copies; and a basic copy rate of 80 copies per minute, about double that of our existing machine. It is black-and-white only. Full specifications are available in Jenny's office. We would like to have your views on this proposed purchase.

And a possible reply:

Well, the copier sounds nice, but I would really like to have that scanner, since I often want to copy news-paper articles into my computer. I've been agonizing over this. On the whole, it seems to me that it would be a good idea to buy it first and to save the other one for next year.

Are you confident that you know what the respondent's view is? This little blizzard of vague pronominal items like *it* and *the other one* leave it largely obscure as to just which machine the writer thinks should be bought first. He would have made everybody's life easier by choosing more explicit words. Perhaps he means this:

On the whole, it seems to me that it would be a good idea to buy the scanner first and to save the copier for next year.

As always, a few seconds of care and attention will pay large dividends.

8.7 HANDING OUT ADVICE

Once you have read and understood everything in this book, you will be a skilful user of email. Your emails will be competent and professional, and they will make a good impression on everyone who reads them. Excellent.

But, of course, there are lots of other people out there who are still far from mastering even the elements of good email practice. They provide useless subject lines, or no subject lines at all. They write all in capital letters, or all in small letters. They fail to sign their messages. Their mails are full of typos and mistakes in English, and are hard to follow. They use foolish abbreviations and cute little doodahs of every description. They demand instant responses, and they give the impression that they regard you as a servant. In short, they get everything wrong.

What should you do when you receive an email from one of these people? Should you grit your teeth and respond to it as though it were impeccable? Should you simply delete it in exasperation and forget about it? Or should you offer the malefactor some friendly advice?

There are no easy answers. Some experienced users

of email have no patience with amateurish fumblings, and they respond to incompetent emails with blunt and sharply worded advice to learn the ropes. Others decline to make any comments at all, for fear of hurting someone's feelings.

The problem with blunt criticism is that it can make enemies and possibly discourage people from using email at all. And the problem with the tolerant view is this: if nobody ever says anything, then the bumblers will never learn that they are behaving badly, and they will go on sending incompetent emails and annoying their recipients for ever. We need to find a middle ground.

To begin with, some kinds of misbehaviour are so serious that there is no point in even contemplating a reply at all: the only sensible course is instant deletion. Among the candidates for this treatment are at least the following:

- Writing in anything other than plaintext
- Sending an empty message with an attachment

Beyond this, I suggest that some sins are so serious that we have no choice: the perpetrators must be warned about their behaviour. Among these sins are at least the following:

- Sending a message to far too many people
- Leaving the subject line empty
- Writing all in capital letters or all in small letters
- Using text-messaging abbreviations like 'R U' for 'are you'

- Demanding a response instead of requesting one
- Demanding a quick response
- Failing to proofread the message
- Failing to sign the message

I consider that these practices are worse than mere shortcomings: they are offensive and intolerable. If we are going to reply to such messages at all, then we should not hesitate to point out the failings to their perpetrators.

In most cases, of course, we should try to do this as politely as we can. Many of these blunders, awful as they are, result merely from well-meaning ignorance, or even from the corrosive influence of those people who go around advising beginners to keep their emails 'informal'. But one or two of these practices, such as demanding a rapid response, can result from nothing other than sheer crass rudeness, and there is no reason not to say so.

Delicate forms of words which may be useful here include 'You would make my life a little easier if . . .', 'It is considered courteous to . . .', and 'You will make a better impression if you . . .' If you can see a way of framing your comments in such a delicate way, fine. If you can't, well, then you will have to make a judgement: is the blunder serious enough that a blunt complaint is appropriate?

8.8 FORWARDING

If you receive an email from somebody, and you pass on a copy of that mail to somebody else, then you are **forwarding** the original message.

Now, in most circumstances, you must *not* forward mail without the permission of the person who sent it to you. Forwarding mail without permission is extremely discourteous, and it can earn you a good deal of ill will. It is also a violation of copyright, which means that it can get you into trouble (see chapter 10). So, if you think you have a reason to forward an email, then you should get in touch with the sender, explain who you want to forward the mail to and why, and ask for permission.

If you receive permission, then you can go ahead. Your mailer probably has a Forward button, and, if you click on this button while you are looking at the original message, a new window will pop up. The address line of the new window will be empty, waiting for you to type in the address to which you want to forward the mail. The subject line will duplicate the original subject line, but the word *forward* or the abbreviation *fwd* will probably be added. The complete text of the original message, including header and signature, will appear in the window, probably marked off by angle brackets, just as in a reply.

At the beginning of the message which you are about to forward, you should type in a brief explanation of where the message comes from and why you are forwarding it. Failure to do this is inconsiderate, and the absence of an explanation may perplex the people you are forwarding the message to. And you must be sure to place your explanation at the *beginning*, so that your readers will read the explanation before they read the forwarded message.

Naturally, you must make it clear which words belong to the original message and which words have been added by you. The angle brackets should do this automatically, but you would be wise to double-check. And you should leave the original signature untouched: *don't* delete the name of the original sender.

Now, as a rule, you should leave the original text undisturbed. Any editing of the text should be undertaken with the greatest care, and deletions should be expressly marked with [snip] or [. . .] in the usual way. Doing anything at all which appears to alter the sense of the original message is reprehensible behaviour. This is a good way to make enemies quickly.

There are just a few circumstances in which it is not necessary to obtain permission before forwarding a piece of mail. One such circumstance arises when you receive a question which you cannot answer, and it is obvious that the sender is eager to find an answer. In this case, the sender will probably be pleased if you pass on the question to other people who may be able to provide an answer. But just make sure, before you forward the question, that there is nothing confidential about it.

Another circumstance arises with jokes. The constant forwarding and re-forwarding of jokes is an everyday fact of electronic life. But listen: everybody gets lots and lots of jokes, and there is no particular reason why you need to forward the latest joke to everybody you can think of.

Anyway, bear in mind that, every time a message is forwarded, it acquires another layer of angle brackets. After six or eight forwardings, the message will contain more angle brackets than words, and the lines will be broken up into barely readable fragments. Unless you are happy to spend a good deal of time deleting that blizzard of angle brackets – and you're not, unless your days are empty indeed – it is best to let the joke die in your inbox.

I will close this chapter with an important piece of advice: *never send a chain letter*. A **chain letter** is a message which asks you to forward copies to, say, ten other people, each of whom will be asked to do the same thing. Chain letters are prohibited everywhere on the Internet, and forwarding a chain letter may well get you banned from the Net. If a chain letter arrives in your inbox, you should notify your system administrator: your Internet service provider, your employer or your university, as the case may be. The same goes if you receive anything which appears to be illegal.

> *Chapter summary:*
> - Carefully check the addresses you are replying to
> - Delete all unneeded material
> - Reply point by point, so far as possible
> - Be sure you have replied to all points required
> - Do not forward mail without permission

9

Posting to Mailing Lists and Newsgroups

9.1 WHAT IS A LIST?

A **mailing list** is a service allowing subscribers to exchange emails on a particular topic. There are thousands of lists out there, so many that I don't even know how to find out how many there are, though tens of thousands of lists are listed at http://list.com. Many lists are aimed at professionals who specialize in a particular area, and they do not welcome beginners, but many other lists are more informal, and are open to anybody who is interested. There are lists devoted to almost any area that might be studied in a university: Slavic languages, asteroids, place names, evolutionary psychology . . . well, you get the picture. And, of course, there are lists devoted to non-academic interests.

I happen to be a professional linguist, so I subscribe to the big list devoted to general linguistics which practically all linguists subscribe to. I am a historical linguist, so I subscribe to the list devoted to historical linguistics. And I'm a specialist in Basque, so I subscribe to the list devoted to Basque linguistics, and also to the informal list devoted to Basque culture. In addition, I have some side interests in a couple of other areas of linguistics, so I also subscribe to the lists devoted to those topics, so that I can keep abreast of developments there.

Some lists are huge affairs with thousands of subscribers, while others have only a handful of subscribers. Some are slick professional operations, while others are one-man shows that temporarily fold whenever the owners are too busy to attend to them. Some have lasted for years, while others appear and then vanish a few months later. Some lists are **dormant**, which means that they still exist, but that they practically never receive any messages. A very few lists are private, and membership is by invitation only.

Every list has an **owner**. The owner is the person who has created the list, who has arranged the computing facilities that are necessary to operate the list, and who oversees the running of the list. Usually the owner is a single person, but, in the case of a large list, the owner may be a group of people or even an institution.

The name of a list is chosen by its owner. There is no particular system for creating names of lists, but a common procedure is to use a contracted form of the name of the list's subject matter. So, for example, a list devoted to social psychology might be named *SocPsych*.

On a mailing list, we do not speak of 'sending' a message. Instead, we **post** a message to the list.

There are various ways of classifying lists, but a fundamental distinction is that between moderated lists and unmoderated lists. On an **unmoderated list**, every message posted to the list by a subscriber is immediately distributed to all the other subscribers. On a **moderated list**, each message posted is first delivered only to the **moderator** (normally the list-owner), and the moderator then decides whether or not the message should be distributed. If the moderator is not satisfied with the posting, it will be returned to its sender, either with a request for some rewriting or with a flat rejection. I will explain below why these things might happen.

9.2 SUBSCRIBING TO A LIST

First of all, you must be aware that very many lists are intended only for professional specialists in the fields to which the lists are devoted. You should *not* attempt to join a specialist list unless you really are a specialist in the relevant field, or at the very least a specialist in a related field. A specialist list will *not* welcome beginners' questions, and you should not try to post elementary questions to such a list. There are other and more suitable places for beginners' questions.

You cannot post to a list, or even read the messages posted to that list, unless you first subscribe to it. In order to subscribe, you first have to find out that the list exists, and that is often the hardest part. In practice, most people find out about lists devoted to their professional interests by word of mouth, from colleagues in the same field. In linguistics, some of my colleagues maintain a list of linguistic lists, which can be consulted by anyone looking for a list devoted to a particular area of linguistics, and I suppose some other disciplines do the same. Otherwise, you can ask your search engine to look for lists that you might be interested in.

Once you have discovered a suitable list, you need to find the email address to which requests for subscription must be directed. On some lists, this may be simply the personal address of the list-owner, but more usually there is a separate address, directed to the **list-server**, the computer which manages the business of the list. This address usually begins with the sequence 'listserv', or sometimes **major-domo**. You will receive instructions for subscribing, which will typically involve no more than sending in your name and your email address in a specified format. Once the list-server has accepted your request to subscribe, you are a member of the list. That means that you will receive the messages posted to the list, and that you can post messages yourself.

As soon as you subscribe to a list, you will be sent a page or two of instructions about how to use that list. Among other things, you will be told how to subscribe, how to unsubscribe (this awkward word is now standard), and how to suspend your subscription temporarily when you're away, using the Nomail option. Now, here is some valuable advice: *keep a copy of these pages.* According to taste, you can copy them into a file on your computer, or you can print them out and put the printed pages into a ring binder which you keep handy. But, whichever you prefer, make sure you keep this information where you can find it quickly. If you don't, you will eventually regret it, and you will wind up wasting a good deal of time in trying to find out something which is explained in these pages.

There is one thing which you absolutely must understand from the outset. Every list has two addresses. One is the address of the list-server, to which messages involving subscriptions must be directed. The other is the address of the list itself, to which messages must be posted for distribution. You must keep track of both addresses, and you must remember which is which. It is all too common to see bewildered subscribers sending 'unsubscribe' messages to the list, which is a futile waste of time for all concerned. This is one reason why you must keep a copy of those pages of information.

Some busy lists offer a **digest** service. If you choose the digest option, then you won't receive every message when it is posted. Instead, about once a week, you will receive a summary of that week's postings, and you can choose which ones you want to look at. The point of the digest is to keep your inbox from being inundated with postings. I don't use the digest service, but my colleagues who do use it report varied experiences. Some digests apparently work smoothly, while others deliver postings in the form of attachments (discussed in chapter 6), and these attachments, as always, may be difficult or impossible to open.

9.3 PROTOCOL

Included in those pages of information which I have just advised you to keep handy will probably be some guidelines on list protocol. *Check those guidelines; remember them, and follow them.* It is the list-owners who are undertaking all the trouble of setting up and maintaining the lists, and they are providing this service for free. They therefore have an absolute right to require subscribers to behave in a specified manner. If you don't like the list-owner's rules, then you should get off the list. You can always set up your own list with your own rules, you know.

The first point, of course, is that each list is devoted to a particular topic, and therefore only postings on that topic will be appropriate on that list. Most people understand this simple fact without coaching, but there are always a few reprobates who are determined to pursue their own little hobby-horses on any list which will allow them space to do so. Try not to be one of these pathetic creatures. It is really the job of the list-owner or moderator to put a stop to such bad behaviour, but until this happens my advice on how to cope is given in section 9.9 below.

The guidelines on protocol may include advice on how to ask questions, how to reply to questions, and how to present the replies received. In fact, there is a general protocol covering these matters which is now accepted as standard on most lists. This general protocol is described in section 9.5 below. However, if the guidelines for your list say something different, then you must fall into line.

Naturally, the protocol on every list will prohibit flaming, or any kind of offensive behaviour. On a moderated list, any offensive posting will be returned to you at once, at least with a warning not to try it again. A second offence, or even an especially bad first offence, will get you thrown off the list – and deservedly so. On an unmoderated list, your first offence will unfortunately be distributed to everybody, but the list-owner is unlikely to allow you the opportunity to commit a second offence.

On every list, there will be occasions on which you

disagree strongly with the views expressed by another subscriber. On such occasions, it is tempting to launch an all-out attack on the other person. Try to resist this temptation, since fierce attacks will win you few friends and admirers – unless your target is already universally hated, which is possible but unlikely.

When you are criticizing another person's views, it is an excellent idea to find at least one point on which you can agree. If you can write 'I agree with McGregor on this point, but I disagree strongly on these other points', then you will give the impression that you are engaging in a fair and rational discussion. But, if the tone of your posting is 'McGregor is grotesquely and preposterously wrong on every single point he is foolishly trying to make', then your contribution may be seen by many subscribers as little better than a flame.

There is another point, less obvious than most. Lists vary in the languages in which they will accept postings. Some lists are very tolerant, and will accept postings in almost any language which can be typed in the roman alphabet. Others, however, will accept postings only in certain specified languages, which will be listed in those pages of protocol.

Of course, almost all lists accept postings in English, and English is the principal language used on most lists. But there are exceptions. Amazing as it may seem, there exist lists which do not welcome postings in English, and which ask subscribers to use some other language or languages. And there are others in which English is acceptable, but which in practice receive most of their postings in other languages. If you want to subscribe to such a list, then of course you must respect the policy of the list.

Here is a piece of good advice. Once you have subscribed to a list, spend at least a month watching the list, reading the messages posted to it, and finding out how that list works. Only once you have decided that you understand the culture of that list should you try to post your own messages to it. Subscribing to a list and following it without posting to it is called lurking, and **lurking** for a few weeks at the beginning is an excellent idea. Lurking will help you to avoid making a public fool of yourself by firing off an email which is grossly inappropriate on that list.

A message posted to a list is very public. It will be seen by all the subscribers to that list who bother to open it. Bear in mind that these subscribers might include the person who is interviewing you for a job next week. Or they might include someone you don't know now but who you will soon find yourself asking for a big favour. These are excellent reasons for taking great care in constructing your postings. One or two overly hasty or thoughtless postings can quickly give you a bad name, and getting rid of a bad name is far harder than acquiring it.

On top of this, most lists maintain archives of the postings sent to them, so your possibly embarrassing words will be stored for years where anybody can read them.

9.4 THREADS

Very commonly, a posting to a list initiates a discussion, with a number of subscribers taking part, replying to the original posting, then replying to those replies, then replying to those further replies, and so on. A series of postings which are linked in this way is called a **thread**. The postings which make up a thread are linked by their common subject line.

Suppose I subscribe to a list devoted to the origins of language, and I post a message discussing Michael Corballis's recent book on the subject. I might call my posting Corballis's sign-language hypothesis. The responses to my posting will automatically receive the subject line Re: Corballis's sign-language hypothesis, as explained in chapter 8, and the further responses will carry the same subject line. So long as the discussion continues, the subject line will remain unchanged, providing nobody tampers with it.

And you should not tamper with it, in most circumstances. It is that common subject line which enables interested subscribers to follow the discussion without missing a posting, while at the same time they may not be bothering to open other postings on topics they are not interested in. Moreover, that common subject line makes it easy to collect all the messages in the thread when it comes time to put them into the list's archives.

There is just one circumstance in which altering the subject line may be justified. This occurs when the subject of the discussion veers abruptly off in a different direction. Suppose, for example, that one respondent comments on Derek Bickerton's very different ideas, and then several other people jump in with comments on Bickerton, forgetting all about Corballis. In such a case, it might be helpful to change the subject line, and there is a conventional way of doing it. Here is what the new subject line might look like:

Bickerton's sudden-emergence scenario [was: Corballis's sign-language hypothesis]

This is now too long to be fully displayed in subscribers' inboxes, but at least the crucial word *was*
might show up, and the full subject line will be displayed when a subscriber opens the posting.

Even though the repeated subject line will make it
clear which thread your message belongs to, it is still
important to make it clear which particular message
from that thread you are replying to. Hence it is especially important here to identify the sender of that message. The conventional way of doing so is to introduce
the original message like this:

Peter Davidson writes:

And it is likewise especially important to quote at least
a few of the most critical words from that message. As
always, you should not quote the entire message unless
you have a good reason for doing so, but you must
make it clear precisely which point you are responding
to, or nobody will be able to follow your posting.

On a list, it is doubly important to refrain from
allowing undeleted copies of earlier messages to be
tacked onto your own posting. If everybody fails to
delete those earlier postings, then it won't be long
before each new posting on a thread is carrying a
gigantic tail consisting of the entire correspondence so
far. This is grossly inconsiderate of other subscribers,
and it pointlessly occupies a great deal of storage space.

It very often happens that two subscribers become

involved in a discussion of their own. If this happens, then common courtesy demands that they take their discussion off the list and pursue it privately – *especially* if the discussion becomes a little heated. If the private discussion turns up any points that are likely to be of interest to the list, one of the participants can always summarize the discussion to the list.

Finally, if you want to post a contribution to a thread, make sure first that you have carefully read *all* of the postings in that thread so far submitted. You will look foolish if your posting simply repeats what someone else has already said, and worse than foolish if your posting advances an argument which has already been demolished by another subscriber.

9.5 ASKING QUESTIONS AND REPLYING TO THEM

There is now an established protocol for dealing with questions on a list. Unless the guidelines for your list say something different, here is how you should behave when you ask a question or when you reply to one.

Suppose I want to ask a question. Naturally, I must first determine that the list I have in mind is a suitable place to ask that question. Let's look at a real question which I had occasion to ask some time ago.

I'm a specialist in Basque, and I was mulling over the origin of the slightly curious-looking Basque word *lanabes*, which means 'tools', 'tool set'. Nobody had ever managed to come up with a plausible-looking explanation of the origin of this word. The word does not look like native Basque, and it has therefore probably been 'borrowed' (as we say) from a neighbouring language – and the only neighbouring languages are the Romance languages. Of course, I turned first to my colleagues on the list devoted to Basque linguistics, but they couldn't help. I don't subscribe to any specialist Romance lists, and so I turned to the list devoted to historical linguistics in general. There I posted a question with the following subject line: Q: A Romance source for Basque <lanabes> 'tools'?

Note first that I have used the 'Q:' explained in chapter 7. This is necessary, because not all postings on this list are questions. The rest of my subject line is an attempt at explaining the nature of my question as clearly as I can in half-a-dozen words. Then the text of my question looked like this (followed by my signature):

> The Basque word <lanabes> 'tools, tool set' has no known etymology. Its form suggests strongly that it is borrowed. It occurs to me that a Romance plural of the approximate form <las naves> would be a phonologically perfect source, and would also account for the collective sense of the Basque word. But I can't locate any such Romance form. Does anybody know of such a form, with a suitable meaning?

This question should give you an idea of the kind of thing that is discussed on specialist lists. This is not the kind of list that will welcome a beginner's question like Where does English come from?

Now, once my question had been distributed to the members of the list, I began to receive a few replies.

Let's talk about the proper way of replying to a question on a list.

Almost all lists will advise you as follows: *reply to the questioner, not to the list.* So, the people who responded to my question replied to me personally, and only to me. This was easy, because my signature included my email address right after my name.

The point of this procedure is to refrain from cluttering the list with private correspondence. The people who replied were only interested in writing to me, and nobody other than me was especially interested in reading their replies. It would therefore be pointless and thoughtless for the respondents to send their responses to every member of the list. We all get far too much useless mail as it is, and there is no justification for adding to the crowding in anybody's inbox.

That said, there is a minor technical issue here. Not all lists are configured in the same way. So, when you want to reply to a question posted to a list, and you click on the Reply option, what happens? Look at the address inserted into the address line of your attempted reply. On some lists, you will find the address of the questioner – which is exactly what you want. On other lists, however, you will find instead the address of the list – which is definitely *not* what you want. On still other lists, you may even find both – again, not what you want.

Therefore, when you reply to a question – or to *any* posting on a list – you must carefully check to see what address you are replying to. If you find yourself looking at anything other than the questioner's address, then, sadly, you must go to the trouble of deleting whatever is there and inserting the required address, which you can find somewhere in the questioner's posting. (Even if he has foolishly failed to include it in his signature, the list-server has probably found it and inserted it in a header to his posting.)

This procedure is needlessly tiresome, but I can understand that some list-owners prefer to keep reply to the list as the default option. In any case, you must be careful to check, and to amend the address if necessary, since nobody will thank you for cluttering the list with private correspondence. If you find this too tiresome, then forget about using the Reply option, and just create a new email with the right address typed in.

I am not just making a dry academic point here. Several years ago, I posted a question to a huge mailing list. I received a number of interesting replies. But one colleague, for reasons best known to himself, decided to reply to me with the intimate details of his personal problems. He intended to reply only to me, but he failed to check the address line on his message, and as a result 7,000 people found themselves reading the distressing details of his divorce and his ill health.

You might like to know what happened with my question. Several members of the list sent me interesting replies, but they couldn't locate a Romance form of the kind I was looking for. But one member of that list happened also to be a subscriber to a specialist Romance list of which I am not a member. So, he forwarded my question to that other list. And somebody on *that* list came back to me with exactly the Romance form I was looking for. That form was recorded in the twelfth century. And where was it recorded? In Pamplona – which is in the Basque Country!

This little example shows just what a wonderful resource email can be. Before email, my chances of finding that particular Romance form in that particular twelfth-century document in Pamplona would have been very small. I would have needed either the luck of a dozen Irishmen or a fit of inspiration approaching genius. Today, though, I need only to post a question, and within hours scholars all over the world are getting back to me with their own specialist knowledge.

Naturally, I sent a brief thank-you message to each person who had responded to my question. This is standard procedure, and it is no more than ordinary courtesy.

There remains one final step. After I have received the responses to my question, I am expected to post a **summary** to the list. Posting a summary is everywhere considered to be courteous and proper behaviour. So, a week or so after I had posted my question, I posted my summary to the list on which I had posted it. The subject line of my summary was this: Sum: A Romance source for Basque <lanabes>? This example illustrates the conventional format for posting a summary: the original 'Q:' is replaced by 'Sum:', but the rest of the subject line remains as before.

In my summary, I briefly outlined the several responses I had received, drew attention to the importance of that one remarkable response, and then thanked all the respondents by name. This last is important: when you post a summary of responses, you should name all the people who have replied, and thank them publicly on the list.

By the way, there is an important point here. The summary which you post to a list should be a genuine summary – that is, a piece of text which encapsulates the several responses as briefly as possible. You should *not* merely post copies of all the replies you have received, one after another. A compilation of messages is not a summary, and posting such a mess is bad behaviour.

9.6 CROSS-POSTING

If you subscribe to a number of lists, you may decide occasionally that a particular posting is appropriate to two or three of those lists. In this case you will want to consider cross-posting. **Cross-posting** is posting the same message to two or more lists simultaneously.

Be careful about cross-posting. Some lists explicitly prohibit cross-posting, so you must check the protocol for your lists before engaging in this activity. Once again, you will need to have handy those pages which you received from each list when you joined it.

If you do go ahead with your cross-posting, explain clearly at the beginning of your message that you are doing this, and apologize for it. The reason for the apology is that quite a few other people will also be subscribed to those lists, and so they will get multiple copies of your posting. So, if you are cross-posting a message about the names of some of the characters in J. R. R. Tolkien's fantasy novels, you might begin like this:

> The following message is being cross-posted to
> TolkienLang, ElfList and HobbitList. My apologies to
> those who receive multiple copies.

Such apologies are conventional and expected. They show that you are aware that you may be inconveniencing other people.

And, of course, don't cross-post at all without a good reason. If you cross-post all the time, you will win no friends.

One further point. Replies to cross-postings can become dizzyingly complicated. Some people may reply to your posting on just one of your lists, while others may cross-post their replies to two lists or to all three. Further responses to those responses may likewise turn up on one, two or three lists. Before long, it will be impossible for anybody to remember just which comments have appeared on which lists, and people may be bombarding a list with responses to messages which have never appeared on that list. This will delight nobody, and it will especially not delight the owner of the list. If this happens to you, perhaps you can begin to see why some lists prohibit cross-posting.

9.7 SOME NO-NOS

There are a few things which you should be careful to avoid on any list.

Never post merely to correct someone's English. Doing so is extremely offensive, and in the case of a non-native speaker of English it is doubly offensive. Don't even think about trying this.

What about errors of fact? This is more complicated. If the error of fact is crucial to an argument – that is, if the argument immediately fails when the error is corrected – then you are justified in posting a correction. But try to do so as courteously as you can. *Don't* accuse the other person of dishonesty. Instead, try to suggest amiably that he has been misled by out-of-date sources of information, or something comparably innocuous. Correcting errors tactfully is a skill which is well worth cultivating if you want your contributions to be respected and valued by the other list-members. Look at this example:

Calvin Murtaugh writes:

> The first organized set of baseball rules was drawn
> up in 1845 by Alexander Cartwright, and those
> rules thereafter became the basis of the game
> all over the USA.

Well, it's true that this is what all the reference books say, and this is what I was brought up to believe. But I've just been reading Bill James's latest book, and James tells us that the Cartwright story has very recently been dismissed by baseball historians as a myth. For one thing, Cartwright wasn't even in the country at the time he was supposed to be drawing up those rules: he was in England. Well, I'm shocked, of course. It rather looks as though we're all going to have to accept the shattering of yet another of our cherished beliefs. Where will it end?

I don't claim that this effort is wonderful, since I don't think I'm as good at this as I ought to be. But you can see what I'm trying to do: instead of attacking Murtaugh, I'm trying to suggest instead that we have all been misled by poor historical work, and that we're all going to be upset by the latest findings. In other words, Murtaugh is one of us, a fellow sufferer, and not an opponent.

If the error is insignificant, then there is no point in mentioning it at all. Nobody will be favourably impressed by a posting like this one:

Mark Richards writes:

> Though no one realized it at the time, the founding of
> Jamestown in 1612 was the first step in the establishment
> of English as the world's premier language.

As everybody knows, Jamestown was founded in 1607, not in 1612.

Here the small error in the date is of no earthly significance to the point being made, and this posting is as useless as it is offensive.

What about an error of intermediate magnitude, one which is moderately serious but which does not affect the point being made? I can cite a good example here, one that happened to me on a list I was posting to.

I was making the point that any language at all can be standardized and elaborated by its speakers to serve all possible functions, if the speakers want to do that. I chose the example of Finnish, which was formerly only the vernacular household language of Finland, with no standard form and with no use at all for such purposes as education, administration and scholarship. I explained that the Finns had decided to make Finnish their national language, and that they had first created a standard form and then developed the necessary vocabularies, constructions and styles to allow Finnish to be used for all purposes. Fine, but I asserted that this process had begun only with Finnish independence in 1918.

I was in error. A Finnish subscriber mailed me privately to explain that, in fact, these developments had begun in the nineteenth century, before independence. And this was perfect behaviour. My error was serious enough to deserve correction, but it was nevertheless of no relevance to the point I was making. So he mailed me personally with the necessary correction, instead of posting it to the list.

And this is what you should do. If you decide that a correction is called for, send it privately to the person whose words you are correcting, and not to the list, unless you conclude that a correction on the list is unavoidable. I thanked my Finnish correspondent warmly, and you can expect the same treatment.

Don't post merely to express agreement. I do not want to open a posting in my inbox only to find myself reading a message I read yesterday, with I agree tacked on at the end.

Don't ramble. Long and meandering posts are a quick way of losing friends. If you suffer from a rambling prose style, you will just have to put in a lot of work editing your postings before you send them in.

Don't wander off the point. If you get wrapped up in a side issue, then start a separate thread on that issue – *providing* it is a topic which is appropriate to that list. If it's not appropriate to that list, forget it. If you're on a list devoted to medical ethics, and the discussion of a particular case leads you off into a consideration of the behaviour of lawyers in an unrelated case of oil pollution, don't try to shove your views of this unrelated case down the throats of the other subscribers.

Don't ask technical questions about email or the Internet, or about any aspect of computing. If you do, you can expect to receive the irritated reply RTFM, which stands for 'read the [censored] manual'.

Don't re-post your message because ten minutes has elapsed and you haven't seen it distributed yet. Wait for a couple of days, and then contact the list-owner.

Never post an attachment to a list. If the material is too long to incorporate into your posting, then put it into a web page, and post the URL. And, of course, never try to post an entire website.

Never try to post a forgery, not even as a spoof. And don't try to send in an anonymous posting from which your name and address have been removed (though most list-servers won't accept anonymous postings anyway). Make sure everything you post has your name and address on it. If you disregard this advice, it will not be long before you find yourself booted off the list, and with good reason.

Don't try to post advertising. Most mailing lists prohibit advertising. Some will accept advertisements of particular kinds – most commonly, ads from publishers announcing books in the field to which the list is devoted – but only by agreement, and often only in return for a fee.

Finally, don't allow your mailer to send vacation messages to a list. A **vacation message**, or **out-of-office message**, is a fixed response which you can set up on your mailer if you're going to be away from your mail for quite a while – say, for a couple of weeks. This message simply says something like I'm away from my mail until 27 August, and I will read your mail entitled [. . .] when I return. This message is sent automatically by your mailer to every single person who sends you an email during your absence. This is perhaps fine with human beings. But, if you get twenty-five postings from your list during your absence, the list will receive twenty-five copies of your vacation message – and this is going to earn you no friends at all.

If you're going to set up a vacation message, then you should set your subscription to Nomail while you're away, as explained in those instructions which I earlier advised you strongly to keep a copy of, and which you have now probably lost, just when you need them. Otherwise, you should unsubscribe temporarily from the list – but you'll need those instructions in order to do this, too.

9.8 APOLOGIES

Electronic protocol is not so different from everyday courtesy. If you make a mistake, then you should apologize.

One of the most frequent blunders is posting a

private message to the list. It is easy to do this if you are a little inattentive about checking the address line when you click on the Reply button. If you make this mistake, then you should post a brief apology to the list. Posting an apology has the drawback of adding yet another message to every subscriber's inbox, but it is nevertheless necessary. Your apology shows that you have simply slipped up, and that you know you have slipped up, and that you are not the sort of idiot who doesn't understand how a list works and what can be properly posted to a list.

You should also apologize if you discover that you have inadvertently posted something to the list which is seriously wrong. There is no need to apologize for trivial errors, or for errors that have no bearing on your argument. But, if you have asserted something which is crucial to your argument, and which turns out to be false, then you must apologize.

Of course, nobody enjoys apologizing, but failure to apologize in this circumstance is dishonourable and unacceptable. Once you've been forced to apologize for a bad mistake, you will probably begin to appreciate the value of double-checking your messages before you send them. And perhaps you will also appreciate the foolishness of the position I dismissed in chapter 1: 'Oh, email is just like conversation, and careful editing is out of place.'

9.9 NUTTERS AND TROUBLEMAKERS

Sooner or later, almost every list attracts the attention of a crackpot or a troublemaker. We are particularly unfortunate in my own field of linguistics, since language is a topic that seems to attract more nutters than most. But probably no discipline is entirely free of the attentions of these pathetic people. Even such hard sciences as physics, astronomy and biology are plagued by strange individuals who claim that they have carbon-dated the atmosphere, that NASA faked the moon landings, or that the dinosaurs perished in Noah's flood.

What is to be done when one of these people turns up on your favourite list? Well, it is really the responsibility of the list-owner or moderator to exclude crackpots and abusive people, but some list-owners are slower to respond than others. As a result, you may find your list defaced for a while by unpleasant or deranged postings which should never have been allowed to circulate.

On the whole, it is wise to ignore such postings altogether. It is impossible to argue rationally with these people, and even the most patient and careful responses to their pestilential messages will achieve nothing beyond eliciting more of the same. However, if you absolutely can't bear to let their rubbish pass unchallenged – and sometimes I can't – then you might permit yourself one careful response. But that's it. Attempting to engage in a debate with one of these people will merely waste large chunks of your time.

If the list-owner appears to be slow in recognizing

the problem, a private approach might be in order. Some of the bigger lists have a built-in complaints procedure which you can turn to.

9.10 NEWSGROUPS

A **newsgroup** resembles a mailing list, but it is typically much more informal. Newsgroups are aimed at enthusiasts, not at specialists, and you will be welcome on any newsgroup, so long as you behave yourself. Newsgroups have a different 'feel' from mailing lists. They are sometimes called 'electronic notice boards', because their threads often look more like a series of notices than like the discussions found on mailing lists.

The number of newsgroups is vast – more than 100,000, according to an estimate I saw recently. If you can think of a subject that might conceivably interest at least three people, there is probably a newsgroup devoted to it: the fantasy writings of J. R. R. Tolkien, classic cars, Chinese porcelain, the Kennedy assassination . . .

Unlike mailing lists, newsgroups are named in a moderately organized way. The name of a newsgroup consists of two parts, separated by a full stop. The first part is the **hierarchy**, which is meant to explain the general nature of the groups it contains, such as sci. for a scientific topic, biz. for a business topic, or the celebrated alt. for 'alternative' (miscellaneous) topics. There are about nine big hierarchies, each containing hundreds or thousands of groups. The second part briefly identifies the particular topic. For example, sci.lang is the newsgroup devoted to the discussion of languages and linguistics, while the alt. hierarchy contains such intriguing groups as alt.cows and alt.cheese, whose contents I have not investigated. The names of many newsgroups contain a third element narrowing down the preceding element, such as sci.lang.japan for discussion of Japanese language.

The original intention was to keep the number of hierarchies small, but things have not worked out that way. Today there are thousands of additional hierarchies, each containing anywhere from one group to several dozen groups. For example, the island of Bermuda has its own bermuda. hierarchy, with over a dozen groups dealing with such topics as tourism, politics and property for sale.

Long lists of newsgroups can be found on the Web (look under *Usenet*). Two URLs which publish very long lists of newsgroups are http://www.harley.com/usenet and http://www.tile.net.

Newsgroups differ from lists in a mechanical but important way. You don't send and read postings by means of your ordinary mailer program. Instead, you use a **newsreader**. A newsreader is a specialized program which allows you to join any newsgroups you like, to read postings and to post messages yourself. Some newsreaders allow you to configure (arrange) the messages on a newsgroup to suit yourself. For example, you may be able to set your reader to display only those postings you haven't yet read, so that you don't have to wade through eighty or five hundred messages in a single thread to find the ones you haven't looked at yet.

There are many newsreaders available on the Web, and they are normally free. Some browsers and search engines provide newsreaders as part of their service. Quite possibly your computer came with a newsreader already provided. You are not obliged to commit yourself to any one reader: if you like, you can jump back and forth among several readers.

Once you choose a newsreader, it will ask you for your email address and it will ask you to choose a password (or it may simply assign you a password, but most readers let you choose your own). Then it will take you to an alphabetical list of newsgroups, and you can join as many groups as you like. Unlike what happens with lists, there is no need to sign up separately for each group you are interested in.

When you look at a group, you will find that the postings are grouped into named threads. The name of a thread is the subject line of the first posting in that thread. Depending on how long the thread has been active, and on how much interest it has attracted, the number of postings in a thread can vary from one to a thousand or more.

As a rule, newsgroups are *much* more informal than lists. There is practically no moderation, and very many postings consist of idiotic jokes, wearisome irrelevancies or childish abuse. Nutters and troublemakers flourish on many groups, and the decorum enforced on most lists is conspicuously absent. Many of the stranger participants hide their identities behind pseudonyms. Only a few users bother to delete unnecessary material, and it is commonplace to see a posting consisting of 600 lines repeated from a sequence of eight earlier postings plus one line contributed by the person posting now.

Once again, if you join a newsgroup, it is very wise to watch it for a few weeks before you try to post anything. On the whole, newsgroups tolerate doubtful behaviour more readily than do mailing lists. But you should watch to see what the practice is on the group you have just joined: some groups are more restrained than others.

Newsgroups have a few conventions of their own, not shared with mailing lists. Here is an example. If you are talking about a book or a film, and your posting reveals something important about the plot, then you are expected to include the word *Spoiler* in your subject line, as a warning to subscribers who may not yet have read the book or seen the film, and who do not want to have crucial plot developments given away. Here is an example, involving the film *A Bronx Tale*. If you haven't seen this film, and you don't want to have the ending given away now, then don't read the example:

A Bronx Tale (Spoiler)

At the end of this film, the hero's four friends are horribly killed when their car catches fire and explodes. Their charred bodies are displayed on screen, making one of the most gruesome scenes ever shown in a Hollywood movie.

A peculiarity of some newsreaders is that they may offer you the opportunity of posting only to *some* subscribers. This is done by means of the *distribution* option, which you can set for a particular geographical area, in which case only the subscribers in that area will receive your posting.

Some newsgroups are highly tolerant of postings that some subscribers may find offensive. If you join one of these, and you find yourself offended by the tone of a posting, or of a string of postings, there is probably little point in complaining. You should probably have discovered the nature of the group during the weeks you spent lurking without posting. If you find the postings too much to stomach, you should just leave the group. There is no point in posting just to let other people know you are offended.

Chapter summary:

- When you subscribe to a list, keep a copy of the instructions
- Respect the protocol of the list
- Keep cross-posting to a minimum
- Be unfailingly courteous
- Keep your postings brief and to the point
- Never post an attachment
- Don't allow vacation messages to be sent to the list
- If you make a bad mistake, correct it and apologize
- Don't expect civilized behaviour on a newsgroup

10
Confidentiality and Legal Requirements

10.1 THE LIMITATIONS OF EMAIL PRIVACY

Compared to most other forms of writing, email is ephemeral. But it is nowhere near as ephemeral as you might suppose. It is easy to get the impression that your message leaps directly from your computer to your recipient's computer, and that it vanishes from the universe the moment the recipient deletes it. But this is not so.

Every message you send passes through a series of computers before reaching its destination. Every one of those computers is capable of intercepting, copying and storing your message, and some of them are very likely doing that – not because They are out to get you, but merely as part of the machines' routine backup procedures.

As I write, it has not been long since our newspapers here in Britain were dominated by a story of some peculiar dealings between the wife of our prime minister and an Australian con man. At one point, a newspaper got hold of copies of a number of private emails which had passed between the two, and it published them.

Well, it's interesting that a newspaper can publish private emails with impunity. But the point is this: if the prime minister's wife can find her private emails intercepted and published, then so can you.

Email, in short, is anything but confidential and secure. It is potentially public, and on occasion it becomes genuinely public. So, if you wouldn't want to scc it posted on a public notice board with your name attached, don't put it into an email.

In most countries, emails can be subpoenaed by courts, and they may be liable to disclosure under your country's Freedom of Information Act. In Britain – and doubtless in other countries – the police and the intelligence services intercept emails, and the number of emails intercepted grows substantially every year.

You should *never* email confidential information like credit-card numbers: to do so is to invite serious trouble. Likewise, you should never email confidential or personal information about a third party. Doing so is certain to be a violation of your country's version of the Data Protection Act, and it will get you into trouble with the law. You should not even email another person's home address, phone number or email address without express permission to do so.

If you are surprised that I am advising you not to put another person's email address into your email without permission, there is a good reason for this: some people do not want their email addresses to be generally known. Consider a certain colleague of mine. He went away for a few days, and on his return he found his inbox jammed with over 2,000 spam messages. He therefore changed his email address, and, understandably, he is keeping his new address secret from all but a few trusted colleagues.

And I hardly need mention that emails containing sexual or racial harassment or incitement to violence are serious offences in law. If you are one of those pathetic individuals who believe that 'just kidding around' is something entirely different from sexual harassment, then you will doubtless deserve the trouble you get yourself into.

You also need to be careful about printing emails. If you print a private email on a public printer, dozens of people may have a chance to read that mail before you come along and collect it.

There is another point. Many mailer programmes offer the possibility of keeping a copy of every email sent. Do you know if your mailer has such an option? Do you know if it's switched on? Maybe you should find out. Quite apart from any considerations of security, storing a pile of ancient emails chews up a lot of disk space.

Computers are built in such a way that they keep a record of almost everything done on them. When you 'delete' a document from your machine, all you are doing is removing the link that allows you to recover the document instantly. The document itself is probably still sitting there on your hard disk, and it can be recovered by anyone who has the technical know-how. It is really not very easy to obliterate a document from a computer beyond all chance of recovery.

Not long ago, a university in Britain sold a number

of surplus computers. The university staff had doubt-less 'deleted' all files from the machines before they were sold. Nevertheless, the people who bought the machines discovered that a good deal of highly confi-dential information was still sitting on the hard disks of those computers. As a result, the university is now facing a blizzard of lawsuits for violation of Britain's Data Protection Act, and the financial consequences are likely to be frightening.

Moreover, there are grounds for supposing that email privacy will soon become even less of a reality than it is now. Not long ago, the British government tried to compel all Internet service providers in Britain to make and store copies of *all* emails passing through their machines, in case some agency of the government might want to examine one of them one day. This first attempt was successfully rebuffed by the providers, largely on grounds of cost. But it would be foolish to bet against another and more determined attempt in the near future.

A final point. You may not even own the emails that you send. If you send an email from your computer at work, then your employer probably owns that email. This is true even if your employer has given you per-mission to use your work computer for private emails. If you send an email from a computer owned by your university, then the university probably owns the mail. If you send an email from an Internet café, then the café probably owns the mail. You only own your mail if you send it from a machine at home which you own – but even then your Internet service provider may have some claim.

10.2 LIBEL

The Internet is a diffuse affair. Nobody is in charge of it, and we can seldom declare with confidence that any piece of it exists in any particular location. This diffuseness has for years made the Net something of a free-for-all, with fewer constraints on what can be published than we find in other domains. However, things are changing.

The use of the Internet to promote terrorism, paedophilia and organized crime has induced police forces, and therefore governments, to try to crack down on the much-vaunted freedom of the Net, to suppress some activities and to supervise others. As I write, for example, the British government is preparing to introduce stringent new requirements for Internet chatrooms, in the hope of protecting children from the paedophiles who use chatrooms to attract victims. No one can object to this goal.

But, of course, there are always those who have never cared much for the free expression which has typified the Net. Governments, businesses, and rich and powerful individuals are among those who hate any kind of scrutiny of their activities. Pressure from all these directions has therefore been growing, with the goal of constraining what can be said on the Net. In particular, there is pressure to extend the laws of libel to the Internet.

Applying libel laws to the Net has generally been difficult for several reasons, but especially because of the problem of jurisdiction. Since the Net is not located in a particular place, it is not so easy to determine who has jurisdiction in the event of an alleged libel. This uncertainty has helped to protect freedom of speech on the Net.

But, of course, this too is changing. Very recently, a projected prosecution for libel has been worrying almost every organization and institution involved with the Net.

The case is this. An American business magazine which is distributed on line published an article which was critical of an Australian businessman. That businessman has responded by attempting to sue the magazine's publisher for libel. Critically, and controversially, he has been granted permission by the Australian courts to sue *in Australia* – even though the magazine has only a tiny handful of subscribers in Australia. Why does this matter?

The laws of libel vary greatly from country to country. In the United States, prosecutions for libel are heavily constrained by the constitutional right to freedom of speech, and by a Supreme Court ruling that public figures may not invoke the libel laws in order to prevent scrutiny of their activities. As a consequence, prosecutions for libel in the USA cannot hope to succeed except in the most flagrant cases.

But other countries are very different. At the opposite pole is Britain, whose laws of libel are weighted heavily and disgracefully in favour of a plaintiff. In Britain, almost any remark which is less than admiring can lead to a prosecution for libel, and that prosecution will very likely succeed. Even an *admiring* remark can be grounds for libel if it is adjudged to be sarcastic. A defendant in a libel case in Britain finds the cards stacked against him to an extent which is beyond belief. And, it appears, the libel laws in Australia are similar to those in Britain.

This is why the businessman wanted to sue in Australia, rather than in the USA, where he would probably have no chance of success. And this is why so many organizations, from Internet service providers to the giant bookseller Amazon.com, have banded together to try to oppose what is happening in Australia.

The point of this little discussion is that you cannot now expect to be immune from the laws of libel in your own Internet activities. Even if you live in a country with rational laws of libel, like the USA, the Australian case shows that you are not safe from prosecution in another country with few safeguards for free speech.

So, as the sergeant used to say on *Hill Street Blues*, be careful out there. When you are writing an email, even a private one to be sent only to a single close friend, be wary of writing anything which is critical of any person or organization. I'm not saying that you should never write anything critical at all, but only that you should think carefully about what you are writing. Even describing an obvious nutter as a nutter can be risky. Some nutters are litigious, and even crackpots can sue for libel.

There is one more point. Even in the USA, with its admirable laws of libel, there is a way of crippling somebody who says rude things about you. Suppose you publish an article which is critical of me in the USA, and nowhere else. I now announce that I am suing you for libel. You must now begin preparing your defence, and that means that you must spend a great deal of money. After you have spent a huge sum in preparing your defence, I suddenly announce that I am dropping my prosecution.

Of course, I never had a realistic chance of winning anyway, which is why I am giving up. But you are now stuck. You have spent a pile of money, and quite possibly you are now deeply in debt. You cannot claim that money back from me, at least not without launching a counter-prosecution, which means spending yet more money.

All this is nasty and unprincipled, but it has been done successfully in a number of high-profile cases in the United States.

10.3 COPYRIGHT

Email is not exempt from the laws of copyright. If you didn't write it, then you don't own it, and putting it into an email without express permission from the owner is a violation of copyright, and therefore a crime.

Prosecutions of private individuals for violation of copyright have so far been rare occurrences, but this is so partly because it is not easy at present for authors to discover that their work has been illegally copied into a private email. With the development of new technology, this state of affairs may change.

Things are different if you mail material illegally to a large number of recipients – say to an entire electronic list. In this case your misbehaviour will be obvious to very many people, and it is more likely to come to the attention of the aggrieved author.

The law of copyright allows very brief quotations for reasonable purposes. You are unlikely to get into trouble if you copy one definition from a dictionary into your email – though you must acknowledge your source in full, of course. But copying a dozen definitions from the same dictionary is almost certainly illegal. And copying an entire encyclopedia article will surely get you into trouble if the publisher finds out about it.

If you have never thought about copyright before, the idea is simple: it is against the law to copy someone else's work without permission. This is true even if you acknowledge your source. Observe that we are not talking here about the very different offence of plagiarism, which consists of stealing another person's work and presenting it as your own. The point here is that even open and honest copying of someone else's work is a violation of copyright.

If you are delighted by something you find on Dr Alice Bloom's website, it is fine for you to email the URL of that website to other people who you think may be interested. But it is *not* fine for you to copy a long passage from that website and email this to anybody else, either in the body of your mail or in an attachment. Such copying is a crime.

10.4 DISCLAIMERS

The misuse of email has begun to be seen as a serious problem by business firms and other organizations. If you send an illegal or improper email from your work computer or from your university computer, you will get yourself into trouble, but you will also get your employer or your university into trouble.

This is why many businesses and other organizations now impose strict guidelines on the use of email by their staffs. But many firms have found it necessary to go further, and to add disclaimers to all outgoing email. A **disclaimer** is a statement designed to protect its firm from some types of legal action. A typical disclaimer looks like this:

This email is intended only for those recipients to whom it is expressly addressed. If you are not one of these recipients, and this email has reached you, then you should notify the sender and delete all copies of this mail. The contents of this mail do not necessarily represent the views or policies of the Global Publishing House.

At present, it is not thought necessary for private individuals to attach disclaimers to their mail. But most businesses now consider them essential, to minimize the damage from irresponsible or malicious emails sent by members of their staff. It is, however, beyond the scope of this book to offer advice on this matter. There now exist several books which provide good legal advice to businesses on the management of email, and there are quite a few legal firms which offer similar advice.

Glossary

address See email address.

address book A section of your mailer program in which you can store the email addresses you use frequently, in a manner that allows you to insert one of them into a new email with a click of your mouse.

address line The line in a new email message into which you insert the address(es) to which you are sending the mail.

alias A generic email address covering a number of people. Mail sent to an alias will be delivered to every person included in the alias.

angle bracket The character >, which is used to mark off material which is being quoted from an earlier message.

archives On a mailing list or a newsgroup, a set of files containing records of messages posted to it, usually with some device for searching those files.

ASCII An internationally agreed set of numbers for encoding 128 items: the ninety-five keyboard characters (including the space) plus some formatting commands. The letters stand for 'American Standard Code for Information Interchange'.

aside A comment inserted into the text of an email in

order to express the writer's attitude, such as <yawn> or <hug>.

at-sign The symbol @, which always appears in the middle of an email address, where it separates the username from the domain name.

attachment A document which already exists on your computer and which is copied into a special place in an email, so that the document arrives along with the mail.

bcc line A special address line with this property: any address typed into it will receive the mail, but no recipient will see the addresses on this line.

bounce Your message bounces when it is returned to you with an error message explaining that it cannot be delivered.

broadband A way of connecting a computer to the Internet. A broadband connection is much faster than a connection by modem.

browser A piece of software which allows you to read web pages.

cc A copy of an email sent to someone who is not expected to respond.

cc line The line at the top of an email window into which you can insert the addresses of people to whom you want to send your mail but from whom you expect no response.

chain letter An email which asks the recipient to send

copies of it to perhaps ten other people, who will be asked to do the same thing, and so on. Chain letters are prohibited on the Internet.

compatibility The degree to which one machine or piece of software can work successfully with another.

control character A character which is not included in the ordinary ASCII set, which is therefore not normally present on a keyboard, and which can only be produced by using one of the special keys like Control, Command or Alt.

conversion The process of changing a document from one piece of software into another.

cross-posting Posting the same message to two or more mailing lists or newsgroups.

cut and paste Moving pieces of text from one place to another.

diacritic A squiggle added to a letter to indicate something about its pronunciation, as with é, ñ or ç.

digest On a mailing list, an arrangement by which a subscriber receives only a weekly summary, instead of receiving each posting individually.

disclaimer A formal statement attached to all emails sent from a business firm or other organization and intended to minimize the damage from improper or wayward emails.

domain name The part of your email address which comes after the at sign.

dormant list A mailing list to which nobody is any longer posting any messages.

email Electronic mail, the technology which allows computer-users all over the world to exchange typed messages via the Internet.

email address The sequence of characters which identifies a particular user of email. Example: chris.woods @whiz.net.

emoticon A cute little sideways face created with keyboard characters, intended to express something about the writer's mood or attitude, such as :^0 (surprise) or :-((sadness).

extended ASCII A set of numbers for encoding and transmitting a further 128 characters beyond those encoded in ASCII.

FAQs A list of frequently asked questions, with answers. Many electronic services provide lists of FAQs within their area of interest.

flaming The sending of abusive and offensive email.

font See **typeface**.

forwarding Passing on an email you have received from one person to another person.

FYI: 'For your information': an item attached to the subject line of an email which requires no response.

header A sequence of lines at the beginning of an email message, providing such information as the sender, the recipient, the date and the subject.

hierarchy The first part of a newsgroup name, explaining its general nature, such as sci. (scientific topic).

HTML The special markup language used for constructing web pages. The letters stand for 'Hypertext Markup Language'.

inbox The window on your mailer which displays a list of all the emails you have received and not yet deleted.

Internet A vast network of computers all over the world linked by cables allowing them to exchange information. It is the Net which makes possible email and the World Wide Web.

Internet service provider The organization which provides you with access to the Internet, thus making email possible.

ISP See **Internet service provider**.

junk mail See **spam**.

line length The number of characters, including spaces, which your mailer will allow to occur in a single line before the line is wrapped.

list See **mailing list**.

list-owner The person who has set up a mailing list and who undertakes the responsibility of keeping it running.

list-server The computer which manages the business of a mailing list and to which all messages about subscriptions should be directed.

[long] A caution added to the subject line of an email which is more than one hundred lines long.

lurking Subscribing to a mailing list or a newsgroup and reading the postings without posting anything oneself.

mailer A program (a piece of software) which allows you to send and receive emails, providing you have a connection to the Internet and an email address.

mailing list An electronic service which allows subscribers to exchange messages on the particular topic to which the list is devoted.

mail spool See **inbox**.

major-domo See **list-server**.

modem A device which allows a computer to be connected to the Internet by means of an ordinary telephone line.

moderated list A mailing list which is organized so that each posting submitted is first scrutinized by a moderator, who decides whether or not it should be distributed to the list.

moderator On a moderated list, the person who supervises the list and decides which messages should be posted.

Net See **Internet**.

Netiquette The set of rules constituting courteous and proper behaviour in email, and on the Internet generally.

newsgroup An electronic service which is similar to a mailing list but less formal, and which must be accessed with a newsreader.

newsreader A piece of software which allows you to read postings on newsgroups and to post to those groups.

on line You are on line when your computer is connected to the Internet.

out-of-office message See **vacation message**.

owner See **list-owner**.

plaintext Ordinary text, consisting only of the ninety-four standard keyboard characters and the space, with no control characters.

post To post a message is to send it to a mailing list or a newsgroup.

preferences The section of your mailer program which allows you to arrange features of your mail to suit your taste.

protocol On a mailing list or a newsgroup, the set of rules governing proper behaviour.

Q: An item attached to the beginning of the subject line of an email which is a question.

Re: An item whose presence at the beginning of a subject line shows that the current message is a reply to an earlier message.

Req: An item attached to the beginning of the subject line of an email which is a request.

RichText A simple format into which word-processed documents can be converted in order to minimize the difficulty of opening and reading them.

salutation The (optional) opening greeting in an email, such as Dear Mike.

search engine A piece of software which allows you to search the Web for pages on a particular topic.

.sig See **signature** (sense 2).

signature 1. The name (and possibly other information) which you place at the end of your emails. 2. The section of your mailer program which allows you to construct such a signature.

smiley The character ;-), which indicates that the material preceding it is a joke. (Note: some people use the term 'smiley' more generally, as a label for any emoticon.)

snail mail Ordinary paper mail, the kind delivered by the post office.

[snip] An item inserted into a quoted message to show that material has been deleted.

spam Electronic junk mail: mail from strangers whose purpose is to extract money from you, honestly or dishonestly.

subject line The line at the top of an email which announces its subject.

Sum: An item whose presence in a subject line indicates

that the current message is a summary of the responses to an earlier question.

summary A message posted to a mailing list summarizing the responses to a question asked earlier.

thread On a mailing list or a newsgroup, a series of related postings on a common topic, normally united by a common subject line.

typeface A particular style of type – in other words, a particular way of shaping the letters of the alphabet and the other characters which appear on the screen.

Unicode A system which allows software to display thousands of characters, including for example phonetic symbols and Chinese characters.

unmoderated list A mailing list which is organized so that every posting to it is immediately distributed to all subscribers, without scrutiny.

URL The address of a web page. The letters stand for 'Universal Resource Locator'.

username The part of your email address that comes before the at-sign.

vacation message A message which you set up on your mailer program when you are away from your mail for some time. It automatically acknowledges the reception of every message that arrives and sends out a warning of your absence.

virus A destructive program which causes great damage

to any computer onto which it is introduced. Viruses are carried by email attachments.

Web See **World Wide Web**.

World Wide Web The totality of the pages (documents) stored on all the computers linked by the Internet, plus the programs that allow a person at one computer to read pages stored on another.

wrap When the length of the current line reaches the length limit set for your mailer, the text wraps: it starts a new line automatically.

Index